Venezuela

Venezuela

BY TERRI WILLIS

Enchantment of the World
Second Series

Children's Press®

A Division of Scholastic Inc.

NEW YORK   TORONTO   LONDON   AUCKLAND   SYDNEY
MEXICO CITY   NEW DELHI   HONG KONG
DANBURY, CONNECTICUT

Frontispiece: Hiker climbing Mount Roraima

Consultant: Carmen Madariaga Culver, Academic Director, Latin American Southern Cone Programs, State University of New York–Plattsburgh

Please note: *All statistics are as up-to-date as possible at the time of publication.*

Book production by Herman Adler Design

Library of Congress Cataloging-in-Publication Data

Willis, Terri.
  Venezuela / by Terri Willis
    p. cm. — (Enchantment of the world. Second series)
Includes bibliographical references and index.
  ISBN 0-516-24214-8
  1. Venezuela—Juvenile literature. I. Title. II. Series.
F2308.5 .W55 2003
987—dc21   2002008810

Venezuela

Cover photo:
Fishing boats on
the Caroní River

Contents

Canaima Lagoon

Bird-of-Paradise flower

Venezuela, a Youthful Nation

Local teens spend an afternoon together at Arapo Beach.

Street vendors and shop owners work hard in hope of creating a good life for their family.

V ENEZUELA, LOCATED AT THE northern tip of South America, has been an independent nation since the early 1800s. Its history goes back for many thousands of years. Today, Venezuela is a youthful country. It is home to 23.9 million people, and more than one-third of them are under the age of fifteen. Though they are young, these teenagers have witnessed many changes in their nation.

In 1999 they watched as their country received a new Constitution that rewrote many government functions. They saw a president, Hugo Chávez, who'd been elected by a large majority in 1998, lose popularity during the next four years. In 2002 he was arrested by the military and forced to resign, only to be put back in charge two days later.

The majority of people in Venezuela live in large cities along the Caribbean coast, where teens like to spend time at the beach. In many cases their parents and grandparents had lived in rural areas of the country, like the Andes Mountains or the great plains of the country's center, the llanos. They were drawn to the cities with the hope of better jobs and a better life. For some, that hope became reality—for many more, it did not.

Opposite: **Venezuela's youth**

Venezuelan teenagers have seen their country's economy go from bad to worse. They live in a nation where 67 percent of the population exists below the poverty level. However, many don't think of themselves as poor. During the years when the teens' parents were teenagers themselves, Venezuela was the wealthiest nation in South America. Most people got used to enjoying the good life and refuse to give it up today. Young people in Venezuela may live in crowded apartments, but they love to shop and enjoy the newest music and the latest fashions.

Venezuelan teenagers speak Spanish as their main language, but most have learned a little English, too. Almost all of them are Catholic, but only a small percentage of them attend mass on Sundays. They place a high priority on education, and most go to school through age eighteen. The country has several good universities for those who are able to continue further with their education.

During their free time teens in Venezuela enjoy many of the same activities that teens in North America do. Watching television, especially soap operas, is a popular pastime. The favorite spectator sport is baseball, and Venezuelan fans follow their favorite players in the Venezuelan league and in the U.S. major leagues. They enjoy many kinds of music, most of it with a fast and heavy beat that makes dancing fun!

Teens in Venezuela, just like teens throughout the world, hope for a prosperous future, a peaceful nation, and freedom to make their own choices. Will a life in Venezuela be able to grant them these things? It's impossible to say for sure, but a better understanding can be gained by learning more about

VENEZUELA
- Cities of over 50,000 people
- Smaller cities and towns
- National Parks

0 ————— 60 miles
0 ————— 90 kilometers

CARIBBEAN SEA

NETHERLANDS ANTILLES
Aruba
Curacao   Bonaire   DEPENDENCIAS FEDERALES
Los Roques   El Roque   Testigoes   Grenada
Tucuyo R.   Tortuga   Isla de Margarita   Tobago   TRINIDAD & TOBAGO
Gulf of Venezuela   Puerto Cabello   Trinidad
Coró   Caracas
Maracaibo   San Felipe   Puerto la Cruz
Cabimas   Barquisimeto   Valencia   Maracay   Barcelona
Ciudad Ojeda   Chivacoa   Guanipa R.
Trujillo   San Carlos   Tucupita
Acarigua   Ciudad
Mérida   Barinas   Guárico R.   Bolívar   Ciudad Guayana
Apure R.   Orinoco R.
Táriba   San Fernando   Guri Dam   Cuyuni R.
Arauca R.   Caura R.   Coroni R.   GUYANA
Meta R.   R. Carrao   DISPUTED AREA
Angel Falls

Puerto Ayacucho

COLOMBIA   Orinoco R.   Guana

BRAZIL

N
W   E
S

Venezuela

Venezuela's history, its great natural resources, its struggling economy, and the lives of the people who call this nation home.

Paradise on Earth

PARADISE ON EARTH. THAT IS HOW CHRISTOPHER COLUMBUS described the land that is now Venezuela when he became the first European to set foot there, in 1498. Millions of residents and visitors in the centuries since then have also enjoyed Venezuela's diverse landscapes.

This land—with the beautiful white sands of its long Caribbean coastline, the stunning peaks of the Andes Mountains, the vast grasslands of the country's interior, the Orinoco River and its glistening waterfalls, and the colorful rain forests of the southeast—is a kaleidoscope of scenic landscapes.

Opposite: **Waterfall in Puerto la Cruz's Parc la Sirena**

Hacha Falls in Canaima National Park

The Caracas Islands are just a few of the many islands off Venezuela's coast.

Venezuela is at the northern tip of South America. With the Caribbean Sea to its north, Venezuela has 1,736 miles (2,800 kilometers) of coastline. More than 300 islands and keys are part of Venezuela, too, although most are tiny. Only Isla de Margarita is substantial. To the west is Colombia, Brazil is to the south, and Guyana is to the east. Venezuela encompasses 352,143 square miles (912,050 square kilometers), slightly more than twice the size of California. It has twenty-two states, one federal district, and one federal dependency. Most of the residents have crowded into the coastal areas, leaving much of the inland barely populated.

Venezuela is considered to be a part of Latin America. These are the countries of the Western Hemisphere, south of the United States, where Spanish, Portuguese, or French are the official languages. Spanish is the official language of Venezuela.

Geographical Regions

Geographers have different methods of classifying and organizing Venezuela's diverse lands. Some break the country up into six or seven different regions; others, only four. However the regions are categorized, these are only interpretations—the different regions are not defined in any political sense. No matter how geographers group the physical features of Venezuela's lands, the end result is the same: it is a vast and varied nation, with amazing landscapes and plentiful resources.

One common way to categorize Venezuela's geography is into five categories: the Andes, the coast, the Maracaibo Lowlands, the llanos, and the Guayana Highlands.

Soaring peaks of the Andes

The Andes Region

The Andes Region contains mountains in the range that extend north and east from the Andes Mountains in Colombia. The mountains are higher inland, losing some altitude as they stretch along the coast.

The Andes Range stretches 4,500 miles (7,242 km) across South America, from its southern tip north to the Caribbean coast in Venezuela. The range splits into two ranges in Colombia. One range, the Sierra de Perijá, continues northward. The other range, the Cordillera de Mérida, arcs north and east across Venezuela.

The city of Mérida is a main population center in this region. It is home to about 220,000 people. High on a plateau, along the Chama River, Mérida has as its backdrop the five highest peaks in the Venezuelan Andes. The world's longest and highest cable car takes riders through some of this spectacular scenery. Starting in Mérida, the ride is some 7.5 miles (12.5 km) long, and reaches an altitude of 15,630 feet (4,765 meters). It takes about an hour, and those who make the trip to the top are afforded a magnificent view of the city and the surrounding area.

Lands known as the Segovia Highlands are also a part of the Andes Region. This area of low hills and plains, located in northwest Venezuela, is fairly dry but still a productive agricultural region. Sugar and cocoa plantations flourish. Copper mining is another important part of the economy here, and has been since copper was first discovered in 1605. Barquisimeto, Venezuela's fourth-largest city, with a population of 602,450, was founded here as a mining community.

Segovia Highlands

The Coastal Region

The coastal region is found along the Caribbean Sea, and for a small eastern portion, also along the Atlantic Ocean. The coastal strip is thin, only a few miles wide in most places. Inland, the land sweeps up into the steep, heavily forested mountain range. It was difficult for early explorers to cross further into the country, so many of the early Spanish settlements were on the coast. Today, some of these early settlements have developed into modern communities.

Though it is Venezuela's most densely populated area, the coastal region covers only 3 percent of the country. Venezuela's capital, Caracas, is located near the coast, along with several other large cities. These cities have flourished in the fertile areas between the mountains and coast.

Venezuelan coastline at Playa Grande

The Flooding of 1999

One of the greatest natural disasters to hit Venezuela occurred during December 1999 along the central coast, a stretch often referred to as El Litoral. Torrential rains did great damage to this beautiful area where the beach is a thin strip of warm sand between the Caribbean and the mountains of El Ávila National Park to the south. The rains began in the south. In the mountains, mild streams filled with water and became ferocious rivers. As these rivers rushed to the sea, they carried dirt, trees, and giant boulders with them, washing out everything in their paths. From the north, the storms churned the waters of the sea. The beach was pounded with torrents of water from both directions. Homes and businesses were destroyed along with the beautiful vegetation. This had been a densely populated area with many extraordinary mansions, but also thousands of congested slum dwellings. Billions of dollars of property were lost, and no one knows for sure how many people died, though estimates range from 30,000 to as many as 200,000. Aid poured in from around the world, but the rebuilding process has been slow.

The coastal region is a popular tourist spot, attracting visitors with its palm-fringed sunny beaches. The tropical islands off the coast are also included as part of this region. The largest, Isla de Margarita, has several cities and is the nation's premier vacation destination. Back on the mainland, the most beautiful and accessible beaches are found in the Mochima National Park. Fringed with palm trees that shade the white sands, these beaches are great spots for snorkeling and scuba diving.

Tourism isn't the only economic activity here. Puerto la Cruz, once a small fishing village, has grown to become a major international oil shipping port. La Guaira and Puerto Cabello are also important ports. Naricual, near the coast, has a major coal mine.

The Maracaibo Lowlands Region

The Maracaibo Lowlands is the region surrounding Lake Maracaibo. With the Sierra de Mérida and the Perijá range flanking the lake, there is very little wind here, and it's one of the hottest areas in South America. The average year-round temperature is 82° Fahrenheit (28° Celsius). Because of the heat, most residents start their daily activities at dawn. Things slow down at midday when most take a long break for lunch and relax away from the heat. Then, around 3:00 P.M., they resume their chores.

At the foot of the mountains, rocks and sand surround the lake. Lake Maracaibo is 133 miles (214 km) long and 62 miles (99 km) wide. The largest lake in South America, it has a narrow strait that empties into the Gulf of Venezuela in the

Little Venice

The name Venezuela was given by Amerigo Vespucci, an Italian explorer who landed along the country's Caribbean coast in 1499, the year after Christopher Columbus first visited. The native tribes who inhabited the area, the Carib and Arawak Indians, lived in little thatched houses built on stilts over the water near the beaches. The explorer was reminded of the Italian city of Venice which is also built on the water. He called the new land Venezuela, "Little Venice."

Caribbean Sea. During high tide, ships are able to pass through into the lake.

Beneath Lake Maracaibo are vast oil deposits, discovered in the early 1900s. They are some of the most extensive in the world. Along its eastern shore, in particular, thousands of wells dot the plains, and thousands more are seen on the surface of the lake. This is the center of activity for all the oil production in Venezuela, an important part of the country's economy.

Oil drilling operations on Lake Maracaibo

Looking at Venezuela's Cities

With a population of 1,207,513, Maracaibo (below) is Venezuela's second largest city. It began as a port, an important link between the Andean states and the coast. Here, such riches as gold and silver, along with valuable coffee beans, were loaded onto ships. This precious cargo made Maracaibo famous. The city has a long history of fending off pirates who were after these goods. Today, the port mainly ships out another valuable product, oil.

Valencia, population 903,706, is the third largest city in Venezuela. Though founded as a city in 1555, indigenous groups have actually inhabited the area for more than 4,000 years. Some of those early inhabitants left behind petroglyphs, known as *piedras pintadas*, or "painted rocks." Many can be seen at Piedras Pintadas Park, just outside Valencia. The city is now considered the manufacturing capital of Venezuela.

One of Venezuela's oldest cities is Barquisimeto, founded in 1552. Today, with a population of 602,450, it is the fourth largest city in the country. It is home to one of the largest wholesale produce markets in South America. The fruits, vegetables, and grains sold here supply more than 60 percent of Venezuela's needs, and are transported to many other countries as well.

Ciudad Guayana, population 536,506, is Venezuela's fifth largest city and is one of the nation's youngest. It was established in 1961, when the cities of Puerto Ordaz and San Félix were joined to help promote industrial development in the Guayana Region. Large iron ore, steel, and aluminum plants support the economy here. These products can be loaded onto ships and transported to the Caribbean Sea on the Orinoco River.

An egret wades upon the flooded llanos during the rainy season.

The llanos, or plains, are the great treeless lands of the Orinoco River Valley, found between the Venezuelan and the Guayana Highlands. Low-lying and wet, they are about 600 miles (968 km) long, and 200 miles (323 km) across. They cover nearly a third of the country. It is a challenging environment, with poor soil. The numerous streams and rivers that flow through the llanos are prone to flooding during the rainy winter season from May to October, and drought (little or no rain) is common during the dry summer months of November to April.

It is a good region for raising cattle, though. Most of Venezuela's 16 million cattle are raised here. The human population, however, is only about 10 percent of the nation's total. These wide-open spaces are barely touched by humans. Historically, it was home to mostly missionaries and cattlemen. Today, ranchers inhabit the area. More residents work in the oil fields in the east and central llanos, while others are working on building dams to control the annual flooding and provide irrigation. These recent projects have enabled the llanos to be used for more than half of the nation's corn and rice production.

The llanos are vast—flat and wide open—and visitors to the region often find them to be quite beautiful. They are not as striking as most of Venezuela's landscape, but memorable, still. The sight of cowboys on the plains, or of the great variety of birds and other wildlife here, make the llanos a special place.

The Orinoco River

The Orinoco River, all 1,590 miles (2,560 km) of it, flows within Venezuela, mostly in the llanos. The river and its many tributaries make up the third largest river system in South America. It flows in an arc, beginning at an altitude of 3,523 feet (1,073 m). There, it is a mountain stream in the rain forest of the Parima Range along the border of Venezuela and Brazil. The exact source of the river was not located until 1951, and even today, much of the land surrounding the Orinoco's headwaters remains unexplored. From the rain forest, the river flows slightly northwest, then gracefully curves to the northeast, picking up water from the wet llanos before spilling out into the Atlantic at the site of its great delta. Along the way it is joined by many tributaries.

Throughout its course the Orinoco River is an average of 4 miles (6 km) wide. It is navigable, or deep and wide enough for oceangoing ships to travel on it, some 260 miles (420 km) from its mouth to the city of Ciudad Bolívar. Smaller boats can travel even farther, for a total distance of about 1,000 miles (1,600 km).

Unlike most rivers today that have been polluted by chemicals poured into them by human development, the Orinoco has remained pristine, clean, and unpolluted. Because such a small number of people live in the llanos near the river, it has been able to stay more pure than most rivers.

The Guayana Highlands Region

The Guayana Highlands, located in the southeastern corner of Venezuela, contain the Bolívar and Amazonas states. This region makes up nearly half the nation. It is a part of one of the world's oldest rock formations—the pre-Cambrian Guiana Shield. Forests are a great natural resource here, and there are underground deposits of iron ore, bauxite, gold, and diamonds.

One of the main cities here is Ciudad Bolívar. It's a port and hub of economic activity. Iron ore and bauxite are mined nearby, so the steel and aluminum industries are major employers, shipping their products out along the river. This city of 225,846 also boasts the only bridge, built in 1967, across the Orinoco.

Guayana Highlands

The Gran Sabana (the great savannah) is a large area south of Ciudad Bolívar. Here *tepuis*, more than 100 of them, dominate the landscape. Tepuis are flat-topped mountains, with sheer cliffs down the sides. They seem to rise from the forest floor below. *The Lost World*, a novel about prehistoric times come to life, was written by Sir Arthur Conan Doyle after he was inspired by the primitive landscape of the area.

The largest tepui, Auyántepui, is 270 square miles (700 sq km) on top. Angel Falls, the world's highest waterfall, plunges off the side of Auyántepui. It is 3,212 feet (979 m) high—sixteen times higher than Niagara Falls. When water leaves the top of Angel Falls, it drops for fourteen seconds before it reaches the bottom!

A tepui towers over the Gran Sabana

Angel Falls History

Deep in the heart of the Gran Sabana, Angel Falls was a secret known only to the local Indians. It went unknown to white men until 1910, when Venezuelan explorer Ernesto Sánchez La Cruz sighted it. It was later named after American bush pilot Jimmy Angel. He first landed atop Auyántepui in 1921 with a gold prospector. Then he saw the falls in 1935 when he flew over it, and went back in 1937, when he crash-landed his small plane near the falls. Luckily he and the others in his plane were able to walk away. The name Auyántepui in English means "Devil's Mountain": a great place for Angel Falls! The Pemón Indians believe that evil spirits inhabit the waterfall.

At 9,219 feet (2,810 m) Roraima is the highest tepui in the Gran Sabana, located near the border with Brazil and Guyana. Its plateau is 44 square miles (114 sq km). Roraima is a Pemón Indian word that means "the large and ever-fruitful mother of the streams." Indigenous Pemón Indians still inhabit the area, and regard the tepui as sacred. They are the only guides authorized by the country to take visitors up the tepui.

Canaima National Park is located here. It is one of the six largest national parks in the world, and its 7.4 million acres (3 million hectares) overlap much of the Gran Sabana.

Hidden among the tepuis is the lovely little Canaima Lagoon—a beach-lined natural pool fed by seven waterfalls that tumble into it from the Rio Carrao. The lagoon is one of the most popular tourist destinations in the area.

A major controversy erupted late in the 1990s when the Venezuelan government supported a plan to build a 470-mile (756 km) power line through Canaima Park. Power would come from the Guri Hydroelectric Dam on the Caroní River. Built in 1963, the Guri Dam is one of the world's largest dams. It supplies 70 percent of Venezuela's electric needs. The new power line would enable Venezuela to sell electricity to Brazil and provide power for increased gold mining and logging in the area.

The Pemón were angry that they were not consulted, even though the power line would cross their land. They feared that the project would damage the land, and with it, their way of life. Construction began in 1998, and throughout the next two years the Pemón, along with other indigenous groups, staged many protests. They interrupted traffic, stopped construction

Waterfalls tumble into Canaima Lagoon

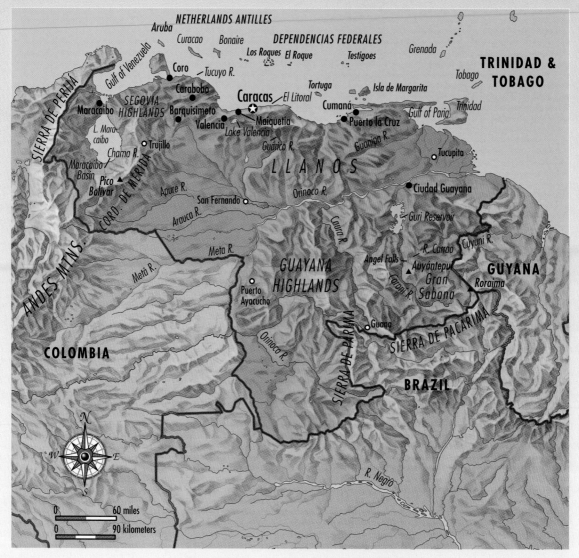

Venezuela's Geographical Features

Area: 352,143 square miles (912,050 sq km)

Greatest Distance North to South: 790 miles (1,271 km)

Greatest Distance East to West: 925 miles (1,489 km)

Land and Water Borders: to the north, the Caribbean Sea; to the west, Colombia; to the south Brazil; to the east, Guyana

Highest Elevation: 16,427 feet (5,007 m) at Pico Bolívar

Lowest Elevation: Sea level along the coastline

Length of Coastline: 1,736 miles (2,800 km)

Highest Average Temperatures: 69°F (21°C) in Caracas; 85°F (29°C) in Maracaibo

Lowest Average Temperature: 65°F (18°C) in Caracas: 81°F (27°C) in Maracaibo

Average Annual Precipitation: 33 inches (84 cm) in Caracas; 23 inches (58 cm) in Maracaibo.

crews, and toppled huge steel towers that the workers had erected. They demanded to meet with Venezuelan President Hugo Chávez. In 2000 an agreement was reached and the Pemón allowed the power line to be built. In return, Chávez agreed to set up a commission to study the land claims of Venezuela's indigenous people, to fund social and economic projects for them, and to ban further industrial development in the region.

Climate

Venezuela's landscape is different in each region and so is the climate. At high altitudes in the Andes, snow covers the ground year-round. For most of the country the climate is tropical and comfortable. Temperatures rarely vary by more than a few degrees from season to season. The coastline is influenced by the trade winds. The northeastern trade winds bring dry air in the summer months from April to November. This period is actually the cooler time of the year. The rainy season is winter, from May to October, when temperatures are a few degrees warmer. Rains, at least in the northern part of the country, are usually brief intense downpours in the afternoon, followed by quickly clearing skies.

Rainfall increases farther south, over the llanos and Guayana Highlands. Here, about 59 inches (150 cm) fall each year, mostly during the winter. The heaviest rainfall in Venezuela occurs in the Amazonas, Bolívar, and Delta Amacuro states, in the Guayana Highlands region. Falcón is the driest state, and the city of Coro hardly ever gets rain.

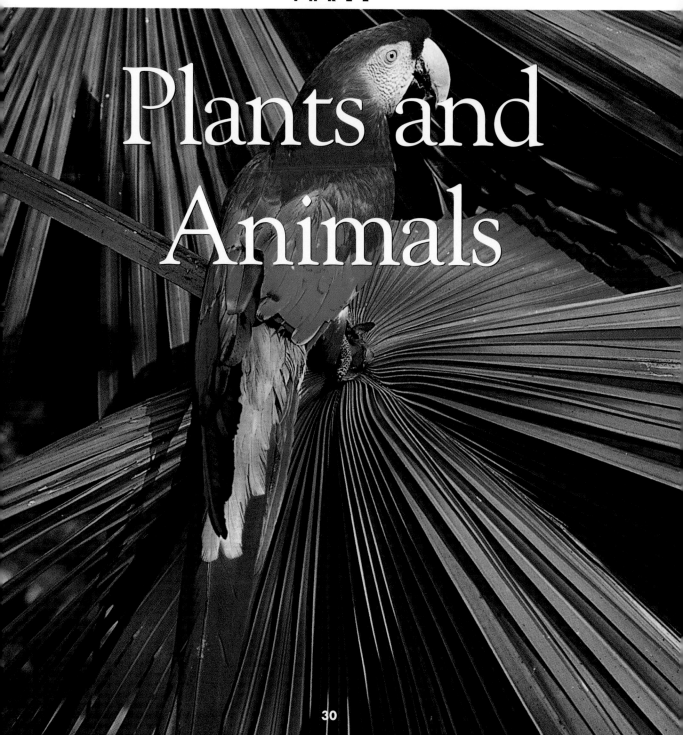

Plants and Animals

W

ITH ALL THE BEAUTIFUL AND DIFFERENT LANDSCAPES and environments Venezuela holds within its borders, it is no surprise that there are a large number of plants and animals living there, too.

Opposite: **A scarlet macaw, vivid with color, perches upon a branch**

Birds

Venezuela is a bird-lover's haven with more than 1,300 species of the feathered creatures. In fact, Venezuela is home to more types of birds than North America and Europe combined! Some, such as the peacock coquette and the velvet-browed brilliant, are found nowhere else in the world. Many birds also find a resting spot in Venezuela as they migrate their way across the South American continent.

The jabiru and the maguari stork, the largest birds in the country, are big and showy. With their long legs they can easily

Left: **Jabiru stork**
Right: **Maguari stork**

Plants and Animals **31**

walk across the flooded plains of the llanos and find fish. They nest during the rainy season, and can have as many as three young each year. There are twenty-one species of heron in Venezuela. Herons are known by their straight bills, long legs, and the "S" shape of their necks while in flight. They, too, move about easily, feeding on fish and crustaceans in the wet plains, as well as coastal lagoons, swamps, and rivers.

There are more than 300 types of hummingbirds throughout the country. These little flying machines have an astonishingly fast wing beat, flapping seventy or more times per second. Because of this, they need to eat nearly constantly, to keep fueled for flight. They lend their brilliant colors to the landscape as they use their long, sharp beaks to snag insects in midair or sip nectar from flowers. They help the plants, too, for the pollen sticks to their beaks and is transported to other flowers. This is an important step in plant reproduction.

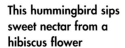

This hummingbird sips sweet nectar from a hibiscus flower

The creatures living in the country's rain forests add distinctive sights and sounds. Up among the branches, colorful spotted toucans fly, and parakeets flutter about looking for food. Macaws, too, add brilliant shades of red, orange, and yellow to the scene.

Along Venezuela's strip of coast, shorebirds, especially pelicans and gulls, are abundant. One of the most common, and most noisy, is the laughing gull. It's something of a thief, swooping down to grab some of the catch that fishermen bring in. It will even steal from a fellow seabird, the pelican. After the pelican dives for a fish and prepares to swallow it, the laughing gull will swiftly move in, land on the pelican's head, pull the fish right out of its beak, and flee with the loot.

Birds fill the air above the llanos, too. Colorful macaws, vultures, ibises, and hawks are often seen. During the rainy season, when the streams are full and the ground is wet, storks, herons, and egrets are common.

Toucans add a splash of color to Venezuela's rain forests.

Feathers of Beauty

The beauty of the great egret nearly became its downfall. Its bright white plumage, with feathers so flowing and delicate they look almost like veils, caught the eye of fashion-conscious Europeans during the Victorian era. The feathers added an elegant touch to hats, creating a fad that became popular throughout the world. The demand for egret feathers caused intensive hunting and trading, and the Venezuelan states of Apure and Barinas were major suppliers. It was here that the egrets nested during the rainy season, under the canopies of the low trees. This environment was challenging enough to keep out most natural predators, but it did not keep out the hunters. The numbers of egrets declined rapidly. Venezuelan egrets were hunted for their feathers until the 1940s, when international laws put an end to the trade. Since then, their numbers have increased.

High in the Andes there are some 600 species of birds. Here, Andean condor soar through the sky. At lower levels the colorful cock-of-the-rock lends beauty, and hummingbirds are numerous when the wildflowers are in bloom.

One bird common throughout the many regions of Venezuela is the yellow-headed caracara, a small hawk with dark brown wings, and yellow head and body. Those that live on the plains are often found walking atop cattle, picking at the ticks that live on the large animals' skin.

Yellow-headed caracara

Mammals

The majority of Venezuela's mammals live in the country's rain forests in the southeast. Among them are several types of predators: foxes and bush dogs, deer, wild pigs, anteaters, spectacled bears, nutrias and weasels, sloths, skunks, and wildcats such as the puma, jaguar, and ocelot. Their diets are varied; the common fox, for example, eats not only mice, but doves and iguanas, as well as fruits such as mangoes.

Bush dog

Giant anteater

A capybara with her young

Tapirs are large wild animals related to anteaters. They can weigh as much as 300 pounds (136 kilograms). The loudest animals in Venezuela may be the howler monkeys, which live in family groups in the upper canopy of the rain forest, swinging from branch to branch. They get their name due to a special bone in their throats, a large hyoid bone that resonates, allowing them to make their loud, distinctive calls.

Capybaras, common in Venezuela, are the world's largest rodents. They can grow to the size of small pigs. They live on land but have webbed feet, so they also do well in the water, making them well suited for life in the llanos.

Dolphins, though they live in water, are also mammals, and three different species are frequently observed off Venezuela's coast. These intelligent animals have adapted well to aquatic life. Their limbs have evolved into strong fins that enable them to move with force and grace through the water.

The Archipelago of Los Roques

The Archipelago of Los Roques is a grouping of more than 50 islands and more than 300 smaller sandbars and reefs that often surface during low tide. Here, some 80 miles (128 km) north of Maiquetía, many animals have found refuge amid the coral reefs and on the beaches. Though it has recently become a target for wealthy tourists, wildlife thrives there because it has been protected as a national park since 1972.

Los Roques is one of the largest marine preserves in the Caribbean. It covers an area of more than 556,000 acres (225,000 ha). Los Roques is home to many iguanas, lizards, and sea turtles. Seabirds flock here, but the unusual and colorful fish beneath the surface of the sea are the real draw. Snorkelers and divers love to see colorful angelfish, parrot fish, moray eel, porcupine fish, and many others.

Reptiles and Amphibians

With all the water in Venezuela, it's no surprise that there are plenty of reptiles and amphibians. The Orinoco crocodile is the largest reptile in all of South America. Slightly smaller, the spectacled caiman is another species of crocodile often found waiting silently for prey at the water's edge or paddling slowly down a river.

The king of South America's reptiles, the Orinoco croc

This anaconda's body swells from a newly swallowed capybara

Emerald tree boa

One of the smallest reptiles is the gecko. Geckos are tiny lizards common in many tropical regions, and Venezuela's coastline and humid rain forest are no exception. They live on small insects, including cockroaches, and many make their homes inside human homes. Others scamper along the forest floor and up tree trunks, filling up on moths, butterflies, grasshoppers, and more.

There are more than 142 species of snakes in Venezuela. About twenty-five are poisonous. Others are also deadly because of their ability to squeeze the life quite literally out of their prey. The world's largest snake, the anaconda, is a constrictor and is found in the rain forest. Boa constrictors also live here.

Among the poisonous snakes are the common rattle-snakes, which usually prey on small rodents, thereby helping local farmers. Emerald tree boas are found high in the upper branches of trees in the rain forest. Its green color makes it hard to see amid the leaves, so it can easily hunt down the birds that perch nearby, using its long fangs and strong jaws to catch its prey. Striped queen snakes roam the ground near waterways, making its meals of the small frogs that hop in the vicinity.

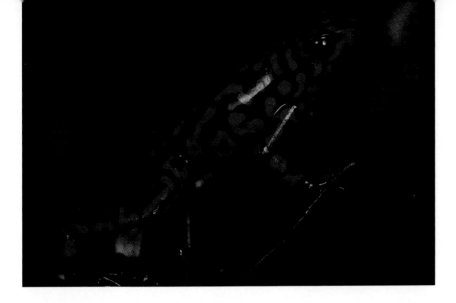

Don't touch this colorful arrow-poison frog—his skin secretes poison!

Arrow-poison frogs are among Venezuela's amphibians. Found south of the Orinoco River, their skin produces a secretion that is poisonous. Native tribes living in the area used the poison on the tips of their darts and arrows. These yellow and black frogs live on the wet jungle floor. Females lay their eggs on the fathers' backs. The eggs remain there until they hatch, and then the tadpoles swim away.

Beneath the Water

Along its coast, and in its rivers and lakes, Venezuela has an abundance of fish. Red snapper, shrimp, clams, lobster, sardines, and oysters are plentiful along the Caribbean coast, as are larger sea creatures: yellowfin tuna, marlin, dolphins, barracuda, and swordfish. The streams and glacial lakes of the Andes are good places for catching trout.

One of the largest fish of the Orinoco River is the cachama, related to the piranha. When fully grown, each can weigh up to 40 pounds (18 kg). This black and white fish has tasty meat and is a commercially caught fish.

Venezuela's National Bird, Flower, and Tree

The national tree of Venezuela is the araguaney (above). The orchid (below left) is Venezuela's national flower, and the country is home to some 1,200 varieties of this beautiful plant. The national bird is the turpial (below right), with bright yellow feathers, accented by black, white, and red.

Plants

Rain forests are home to a wide variety of exotic plants and animals, and Venezuela's rain forest, south of the Orinoco, has its share. Among the most beautiful are orchids, with their big, colorful flowers. The orchid named the Superb lives up to its name. Its lavender flowers are edged in deep purple with a center of yellow and fuchsia.

Helonicas, another rain forest flower, are prized for their beauty, but they have additional value. This plant, which can grow to 20 feet (6 m), has sturdy, canoe-shaped bracts, or modified leaves, that capture rainwater, creating miniature pools. Here, small insects, and even tiny frogs, grow safely to maturity.

Helonica

Bird-of-paradise flower

Helonicas are related to the bird-of-paradise, a striking flower found in Venezuela's Cloud forest. They are a slender plant, growing to heights of 6 to 9 feet (2 to 3 m), with large, exotic orange and black flowers.

Giant ferns have grown in the region for some 300 million years, dating back to the Carboniferous period. Once, the ferns provided food for prehistoric animals. They can be as tall as 60 feet (20 m), particularly in sunny spots. Today, giant ferns grow well along Venezuelan highways.

In the Guayana Highlands, tepuis dominate the landscape. At the top, the climate is cool and wet, and supports few animals, but plants thrive there. The rock that makes up the tepuis is the perfect host for several types of algae and mosses. These small plants, in turn, help break down the rock into soil to support more plants. Many of the plants growing there are carnivorous, that is, insect-eaters, including marsh pitchers and bladderworts. Most carnivorous plants have flowers shaped like deep bowls. These bowls collect rainwater, which attracts insects. Often, the insects will become trapped in the bowl and die. Through its leaves the plant absorbs nutrients from the decaying insect. This allows plants to get the nutrients they need, even when they are growing on poor soil.

Flora of the tepuis

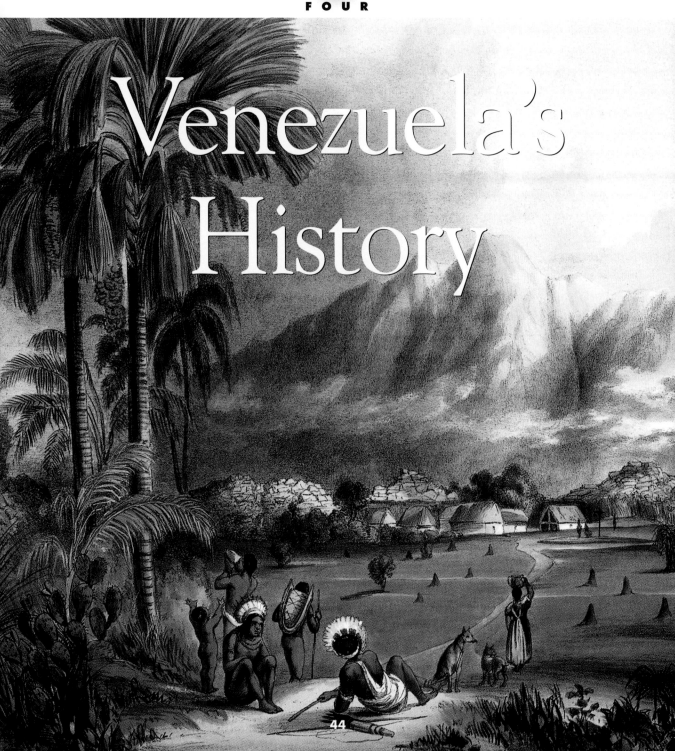

Venezuela's History

THE FIRST PEOPLE IN VENEZUELA ARRIVED ABOUT 16,000 years ago. They came from lands in the east, south, and north. The earliest arrivals probably stopped in El Jobo, in the present-day northwest state of Falcón in the Segovia Highlands. It is there that the oldest archeological finds have been uncovered.

For tens of centuries the various peoples didn't intermingle, or come together, to form a mixed group. Instead, they lived throughout the region and formed hundreds of tribes, each with different laws and religions. Most were hunters and gatherers who found their resources—the materials they needed to live—in nature. They were also nomadic, that is, they moved about in search of food and water. When these necessary supplies were used up in one area, they just packed up their meager belongings and traveled until they found a new home with the resources they needed. They built simple shelters and used rough stone tools and weapons.

Around 5,000 B.C. they began using seashells and bones for tools as well. Seashells were good for digging and scraping hides, for example, and bones were used in hunting. Some 4,000 years later, in about 1,000 B.C., tribe members created pottery bowls and jugs.

Eventually they developed agricultural techniques. They learned to grow the food they needed, so they didn't need to travel to find it. They became sedentary tribes, or tribes that remained living in one place.

Since they didn't need to move, these early people were able to build better shelters for themselves. Once they could grow their food and didn't have to search for it, they had better supplies. They became healthier, lived longer, and had more children. The population throughout what is now Venezuela began to grow at a steady pace. The tribes evolved into several distinct cultures, pulled together by similarities in their location, their traditions, and their languages. The three main groups were the Arawak, the Carib, and the Chibcha.

The Arawak tribes inhabited a large part of Venezuela, including much of the llanos, all the way north to the coast. They farmed in a few isolated areas, growing some vegetables and cotton for clothing. Most tribes in this group continued to fill most of their needs by hunting and gathering resources.

The Carib tribes, who lived along the central and eastern coast, used agriculture to grow some of their food, but also relied heavily on fishing for their meat, and on fruits, vegetables, and animals found in nature. These tribes were warlike and aggressive. Fierce fighters, they would turn the bones of their dead enemies into flutes.

Tribes in the Chibcha group, particularly the Timote-Cuica tribes, lived in the Andes. They were the most advanced, forming settlements that were joined together by trails. They were good farmers, using such techniques as terracing the hillsides and irrigating the soil to grow potatoes and maize (a type of corn).

Christopher Columbus greeted by tribesmen

Venezuela was given its name by Italian explorer Amerigo Vespucci

Spaniards Arrive

Christopher Columbus was the first European to visit Venezuela; it was on his third ocean voyage, in 1498. He anchored in the Gulf of Paria and was greeted by local tribesmen. Certain that he had landed in India, Columbus called the natives "Indians," and the term stuck. Columbus found the natives to be friendly and later wrote that their homeland was the "loveliest in all the world." He was particularly impressed by their jewelry made of pearls and gold, and wrote about it upon his return.

His writings inspired others to make the trip in the search for gold, jewels, and other riches. One of them was Italian Amerigo Vespucci. When he and his sailors visited Lake Maracaibo and saw the natives' reed huts built on stilts in the shallow waters, it reminded him of the canals of Venice. He named the area Venezuela, meaning "little Venice."

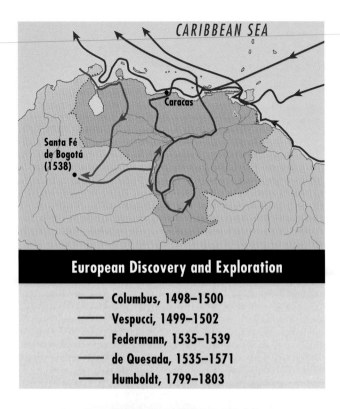

European Discovery and Exploration

— Columbus, 1498–1500
— Vespucci, 1499–1502
— Federmann, 1535–1539
— de Quesada, 1535–1571
— Humboldt, 1799–1803

Spanish explorer Hernán Cortés

When the explorer Hernán Cortés returned to Spain from Mexico with a huge supply of gold, exploration of this New World became even more of a priority. Europeans wanted to find this great wealth in gold they were sure was hidden there, and they wanted to make it their own. They were searching for the mythical city of gold, "El Dorado." Because Venezuela is located at the northeastern tip of South America, it became the most convenient landing place from which to base their explorations.

Spaniards set up a few small settlements along the Caribbean coast, most notably, Cumaná, which in 1521 became the first Spanish town in continental South America. However, they had to fight to maintain these holdings. The natives had been mistreated for years by Spanish slave traders who sneaked into their villages on kidnapping raids. Natives showed fierce resistance to any European exploration into the heart of Venezuela. Many expeditions simply disappeared. Natives killed some, while others couldn't survive in the harsh conditions of the rain forest jungles or the desolate llanos.

Despite difficulties with the natives, Europeans, especially the Germans and Spaniards, pressed on in their desperate search for wealth in Venezuela. Over the decades thousands of Europeans and indigenous people were killed in conflicts. In the mid-1500s, the explorers began to realize that Venezuela probably didn't hold the riches they had dreamed of. Instead, Spaniards began an effort to colonize the land for the Spanish crown. They moved into the Andes and elsewhere in the country, conquering more towns and building roads. Still, the proud and stubborn natives fought every effort.

In 1580 Spanish settlers got a boost: smallpox. The disease was unknown in the Americas and entire tribes of natives were nearly wiped out. The Spaniards took advantage of this and quickly took control of large segments of the region. Spain now ruled Venezuela.

Colonial Times

The period of colonial control is a dismal one in Venezuela's history. Venezuela was mostly overlooked by Spain, as that country focused on its wealthier holdings in Bolivia, Colombia, and Peru. Yet this time also permanently changed the face of Venezuela.

The country's population became far more diverse. Spanish settlers joined the native Indians. Some Spaniards brought slaves with them from Africa to work on plantations along the Caribbean coast. So many Africans were brought in that their numbers were greater than the numbers of the indigenous people. Eventually the three groups intermingled.

From that point on, the great majority of people in the nation have had mixed ancestry stemming from these three groups.

Power, however, remained securely in the hands of the Spaniards. Even though the white Spanish settlers were in the minority, only about 20 percent of the population, they made sure they stayed in control. They did not allow the natives, the Africans, or anyone of mixed race to attend universities, pray in the same churches with them, or even wear the same style of clothing.

Because it was so isolated from the rest of the world, Venezuela, during its colonial period, had a very diverse economy. They could not rely on other nations to trade with them, so they had to produce and supply all the things they needed for themselves. They grew their own food, made their own

Plantations, run by the powerful Spanish, provided food and supplies for daily living.

clothes, and supplied their own shelters. Most of the labor for this work was done by the lower classes of colored and mixed-race people. The profits were taken by the white minority.

As the Spanish flourished, their early settlements grew into the cities of Mérida, Maracaibo, Cumaná, and Caracas. From these cities the Spaniards expanded into the countryside where they established cattle ranches and plantations growing cacao, cotton, tobacco, indigo, coffee, and sugar. Catholic missionaries, too, moved into Venezuela's rural areas, attempting to convert the indigenous people to Christianity. For their efforts, many missionaries were killed. They persisted over decades, though, and eventually they converted thousands.

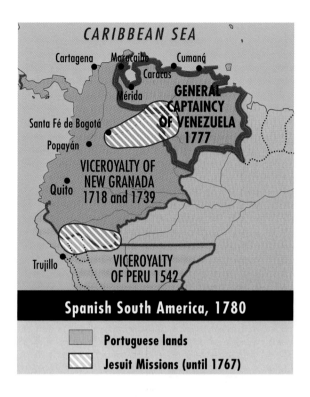

CARIBBEAN SEA

Cartagena Maracaibo Cumaná
Caracas
Mérida GENERAL CAPTAINCY OF VENEZUELA 1777
Santa Fé de Bogotá
Popayán
VICEROYALTY OF NEW GRANADA 1718 and 1739
Quito
Trujillo VICEROYALTY OF PERU 1542

Spanish South America, 1780

Portuguese lands

Jesuit Missions (until 1767)

Venezuela captured the world's attention in the mid-1700s when people throughout the United States and Europe developed a craze for chocolate. The demand for the delicious food was huge, and Venezuelan cacao plantations were in a position to supply the treat. Plantation owners got wealthy in a hurry. The commercial growth of cacao allowed for economic centralization in Caracas. In 1777 Venezuela became a General Captaincy, which meant that it had political as well as military authority. It was a grand time for the Spanish in Venezuela. However, these good times did not last long.

The Fight for Independence

The mixed-race and native people of Venezuela wanted greater control of their own economy. Those most frustrated were the Creoles, the descendants of the conquistadors.

Francisco de Miranda

PLAZA GENERALISIMO
FRANCISCO DE MIRANDA
RECONSTRUIDA POR EL

Though they held much of the local governing power, they wanted more. They wanted to be able to trade their goods with other nations, and they wanted fair prices. The ruling Spanish did not allow this. They limited trade only to the Spanish empire and controlled the profits. Angry Venezuelans began preparing to fight for their freedom.

The time seemed right in 1810. The French army occupied Spain, and the king lost his power. The country was in turmoil. With such problems at home it seemed unlikely that Spain would be able to worry about what happened in Venezuela. In 1810 rebelling Venezuelans ousted Spanish rulers from the country. Francisco de Miranda, a native of Caracas, led them. In May 1812 he was proclaimed dictator of Venezuela.

Venezuela's Independence Day

Venezuela celebrates its Independence Day on July 5. It was on that date in 1811 that representatives from the seven provinces formed Venezuela in a National Congress (pictured). They declared their nation's independence from Spain. It marked the end of hundreds of years of control by Spanish rulers and the beginning of decades of struggle to maintain its freedom.

The seven provinces that formed the new, independent Venezuela on that day are represented today by the seven stars on the Venezuelan flag.

Miranda faced great difficulties, including troops trying to overthrow his government. These troops were mostly made up of the Venezuelan underclass—those of mixed race. Though they were not truly loyal to Spain, they didn't trust a government run by the Creoles either, who already held a lot of power. A lack of funds and government structure also caused problems for Miranda. Within a few months he grew weary of the struggle and stepped down. For this, Miranda was declared a traitor by his own followers and was then captured by opposing troops.

Many of Miranda's closest aides fled the country. One of these was Simón Bolívar. He gathered forces and returned to Venezuela in 1813, beginning what was called a "War to the Death" against the Spaniards. Bolívar recaptured Caracas by the next year, reestablished the republic, and was named *El Libertador* (the liberator) of his country. However, he faced strong opposition from the *llaneros*, a band of soldiers from Venezuela's llanos. They were great horsemen and fierce warriors who were promised riches in return for their fight for the Spanish king. They forced Bolívar back into exile.

Bolívar returned again in 1819 with a plan to bring the llaneros to his side. Together, Bolívar's forces and the llaneros would confiscate the ranches and plantations owned by Spaniards and divide the land among the llaneros. Bolívar's plan worked. In 1819 he was elected president of the Republic of Gran Colombia, as Venezuela was then known. Spain continued to hold parts of the country, but the final struggle for freedom had begun. The Battle of Carabobo, in June 1821, was the deciding battle.

Venezuela was now free, but it had paid a high price. In the eleven years since the struggle for independence began, it lost nearly a quarter of its population in the fighting.

Free at Last

With independence established for his own country, Bolívar attempted to carry out his larger dreams. He had a plan to join all of Venezuela with what is now Colombia, Ecuador, and Panama as one independent state to be called Gran Colombia.

The Battle of Carabobo

Venezuelans celebrate the Battle of Carobobo each year on June 24. The real battle occurred on that date in 1821 during the Venezuelan war of independence. Spanish troops were advancing on the city of Caracas, and Simón Bolívar and José Antonio Páez, leaders of Venezuela's revolutionary army, knew they had to stop them. Venezuela's army consisted of some 7,500 men, including hundreds of British soldiers paid to fight, and horsemen from the llanos. Bolívar and Páez led them into a confrontation with 5,000 Spanish soldiers, in the southwest part of Valencia, on the plains of Carabobo. Fierce fighting erupted, but in little more than an hour it was over. The Venezuelans had defeated the Spanish. Four days later, Bolívar triumphantly entered the city of Caracas. Freedom for Venezuela was ensured.

Delegates from Venezuela, Panama, and Colombia met later in 1821 and agreed to unify, with the capital to be in Bogotá, Colombia. Ecuador would join as soon as it was liberated from Spain.

So Bolívar, even though he was president of Gran Colombia, left to help secure freedom for Ecuador, as well as other Spanish colonies. Eventually, he believed, all of Latin America could be united as the world's largest nation. Bolívar was away for several years in Ecuador, Peru, and Bolivia. While he was gone, Gran Colombia was facing trouble.

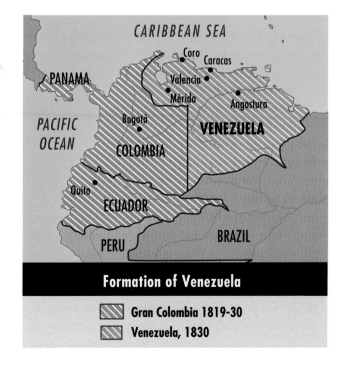

Formation of Venezuela

Gran Colombia 1819-30

Venezuela, 1830

Alexander von Humboldt

Many of Venezuela's natural treasures—its plants, animals, and minerals—were first recorded during the early 1800s by a young German scientist, Alexander von Humboldt. Humboldt was born in Berlin in 1769 and had a vast curiosity about the world. He studied botany, archaeology, physics, philosophy, astronomy, chemistry, and mineralogy. When he was in his late twenties, he used his large inheritance to finance a scientific expedition to South America. He sailed from Spain and landed at Cumaná. He explored the valleys of Caracas and Lake Valencia, the llanos, and then the entire length of the Orinoco River. Throughout these explorations he carefully observed and documented the natural world around him.

Venezuela's largest cave, which he explored, was named for him—Monumento Natural Alejandro de Humboldt. He visited Guácharo Cave and wrote about the oilbird, or *guácharo*, that inhabits the cave, and for which the cave is commonly known. Ten thousand oilbirds live in the cave, each with a wingspan of more than 3 feet (0.9 m). They are nocturnal and leave the cave only at night to find their food, the palm nut, seeking it out by echolocation, or sound waves. Though natives had known of the birds and the cave, it wasn't widely known until after Humboldt's writings were published in 1814.

He wrote about the 24-foot (7 m) crocodiles he observed in the Orinoco, saying they "swarmed like worms in the shallow waters of the river." Of the llanos, he wrote, "All around us the plains seemed to reach to the sky, and this vast and profound solitude looked like an ocean covered with seaweed."

Humboldt spent several years in the area, also exploring Colombia, Ecuador, Peru, and Mexico. He later traveled to Russia for scientific exploration. The peak of his career came with the publication of his five-volume work, *Kosmos*, in which he presented his description of the universe. He died in 1859.

During his life he had many friends and admirers, including the well-known scientist Charles Darwin, who said he'd been inspired by Humboldt. Simón Bolívar said he considered Humboldt to be "the true discoverer of America because his work has produced more benefit to our people than that of all the conquistadores."

Many people in the Venezuelan portion did not want to submit to rule from Bogotá and were ready to break away. Bolívar returned in 1828, resigned from the presidency, and took dictatorial control. Unable to pacify factions, he gave up power in April of 1830. He died in December of 1830 at the age of forty-seven.

A New President

The first president of independent Venezuela was General José Antonio Páez who ruled from 1830 to 1835, and then was reelected in 1839. He had first come to prominence as head of the llanero fighters who agreed to fight with Bolívar against Spain. While Bolívar had been out of the country, it was Páez who organized the country against unity with Colombia. Now, as president, he began to rebuild the nation after the many years of war.

He faced many challenges. During the years of war and struggles many Venezuelans had died. Ranches and plantations were in ruins. The economy was in shambles. Yet Páez was able to bring some stability to the nation. Under his guidance the country rebuilt roads and bridges and kept order despite rebellions that sprang up. He remained in power until 1849, and was then exiled to New York City in 1850.

The decades leading up to the twentieth century were mostly a violent swirl of dictatorships, revolt, and civil war. Power changed hands many times, but it was always kept within the white elite, never held by blacks or those of mixed race. Some good things happened, though. Slavery was abolished and voting rights were granted to all adult citizens. Free public education was established and museums were built.

The central government remained in Caracas, which became increasingly modern, while the rest of the country was rural, holding on to old-fashioned ways. Big changes were about to hit Venezuela with the oil boom!

The Oil Rush

People had known about the oil around Lake Maracaibo for hundreds of years. The native Indians had used the sticky black substance to help waterproof their canoes. Spanish explorers made note of the gooey stuff, but paid little attention to it. It wasn't until the early twentieth century and the invention of the automobile that there was much demand for oil.

A few companies tried drilling in Venezuela around that time, but met with little success. Then, in 1922, a Venezuelan division of Shell Oil began drilling near Lake Maracaibo, and they hit the jackpot. Some 100,000 barrels of oil spewed from the well each day. Before that, the best oil well in Venezuela only produced 8,000 barrels a day. The region around this well was named the Bolívar Coastal Field, and it became famous in a hurry. More wells were dug, and money began to flow into the country. Venezuela was transformed into a wealthy, modern country. The population grew as workers hurried in from other countries, seeking jobs. Many Venezuelans joined the oil industry, too, leaving behind their jobs in ranching, agriculture, and manufacturing. With few workers left, these industries dried up. Venezuela was forced to use its newfound riches to import many of the goods it needed. Oil brought permanent change to the country.

Just before the time the oil boom exploded on the scene, Venezuela faced another sort of explosion—the emergence in 1908 of a harsh dictator named Juan Vicente Gómez. His motto was "Peace, Union, Work." He was able to keep peace, because anyone who disagreed with him was likely to be arrested or killed. The country was also wealthy during his term, thanks to the oil industry. Gómez used some of these funds to improve the nation's roads, railways, and ports, helping the rich oil dealers get even richer. However, most Venezuelans lived in poverty and continued to do so even following the oil boom.

Dictator Juan Vicente Gómez

Gómez died in 1935, one of the wealthiest men in all of Venezuela. He was followed by General Eleázer López Contreras, who was followed by General Isaías Medina Angarita. Both were more liberal than Gómez had been, giving the people and the press more freedom, and helping improve social conditions by funding hospitals and schools and establishing banks. Angarita guided Venezuela through most of World War II. Though the country was not an active participant in the fighting, it did support Great Britain and provided much of the oil needed in the war.

In 1945 a citizen's political party, Acción Democrática, joined with the military to take control of the government. The party wanted to grant further rights to citizens, but conservatives in the country found the party far too liberal and it remained in power only until 1948, when there was a bloodless military coup. Major Marcos Pérez Jiménez, another military dictator, took over in 1952. He had a style similar to that of General Gómez. He put his enemies in jail and made himself very wealthy. By 1958 Venezuelans had had enough. They forced him out of the country and demanded fair government.

The next year the Acción Democrática party returned to power in a coalition with the Christian Democratic party. Rómulo Betancourt was president. Venezuela has had a democratic government since then.

Democracy in Venezuela

As a part of the coalition, the two parties agreed to share power until 1968. In 1961 the government established a new constitution that called for presidential elections every five years. Presidents have been elected from each of the two parties since then. In 1969, for the first time in Venezuela's history, the ruling party peacefully turned over power to its opposition. Both parties strive to better the lives of the country's poor by funding education, improving housing, and boosting health care for all.

In the 1970s the government, led by President Carlos Andrés Pérez, took over the iron and steel industry and then the petroleum industry. This gave the nation's leadership greater control over the profits earned by these economic giants. In 1983 oil prices around the world took a deep plunge. Venezuela's oil profits dropped off sharply. This was the end of the country's oil boom.

Economic difficulties impacted Venezuela's government throughout the 1990s. Today the country struggles to repair the damage from its past. Such things as poor manufacturing levels, dating back to the oil boom; lack of trust in the government, dating back to harsh dictatorships; and inequality among its citizens, dating from as far back as colonial times are issues that the country must now face.

The New Millennium

Venezuela began this century in much the same way as it had spent many of its previous years; with most of its people in poverty and with an unpopular person leading the country.

When the year 2000 dawned, President Hugo Chávez was in charge. In 1992, as a lieutenant colonel, he had led a mili-

Hugo Chávez, president of Venezuela

tary revolt against the unpopular, but freely elected government of Carlos Andrés Pérez. His attempt at taking over the government failed and Chávez was imprisoned for his actions. In 1998 he made a successful run for president. He was very popular with the country's poor people. He promised a complete and peaceful revolution in the country, which would bring greater freedom and wealth to its people. In 1999 his government passed a new Constitution for the country giving the president more control. The Constitution even changed the country's name to the Bolivarian Republic of Venezuela, adding the first word to honor the country's hero, Simón Bolívar. Though it may seem like a small thing, this change cost the country millions of dollars because many official items such as paperwork and documents had to be reprinted.

Within a few years Chávez's plans for prosperity, along with his popularity, were fading. In the early part of 2002 the poor housewives of Venezuela took up an old South American form of protest, the *cacerolazo*, banging pots and pans to show dissatisfaction. When Chávez paraded through the slums of Caracas, where he had once received a warm welcome, the clanging was heard loudly. The symbolism could not be ignored, he was losing friends.

Protests against Chávez continued to grow. In April 2002 more than a dozen protesters were killed and hundreds were injured when Chávez's supporters fired at a demonstration of more than 150,000 citizens against the president. The next day angry military officers arrested the president and forced him to sign a letter of resignation. Pedro Carmona, a wealthy

Pedro Carmona ruled as president of Venezuela for one day only.

Venezuelan, was quickly sworn in as president, but resigned a day later following massive protests by Chávez supporters. Hugo Chávez returned to power. But the protests continued. In early 2003, more protestors were killed. The country was in economic shambles as oil company employees and others went on strike to force Chavez out.

Venezuela's Current Government

V

ENEZUELA'S GOVERNMENT HAS UNDERGONE MANY CHANGES in recent years. Turmoil in the presidency along with an unstable economy has made it difficult to stay on any course of action for long. However, Venezuela is a country with many natural resources and great national pride. The citizens continue in their search for a government that will provide the country with some stability.

Opposite: **Government Palace**

Structure of the Government

Venezuela is a federal republic. It celebrates its independence on July 5, honoring the date in 1811 that the country separated from Spain. Its most recent Constitution was approved on December 30, 1999. All citizens eighteen and older are entitled to vote.

The Venezuelan Flag

The Venezuelan flag features three horizontal stripes of yellow, blue, and red. These are the same colors featured in the flags of Ecuador and Colombia, because for a time in the early nineteenth century the three countries were united as Gran Colombia. Each of the colors in the Venezuelan flag has a special meaning. Yellow represents the gold, or wealth, of the country. Blue stands for the water over which Spanish explorers traveled to settle the new land. Red is for the blood lost by the thousands who died during the many decades the country fought for its independence.

The seven stars in an arc in the blue field represent the seven Venezuelan provinces that, in 1811, were liberated from Spain.

National Assembly in session

Venezuela's federal government is divided into five powers, similar to branches: the executive, the legislative, the judicial, the electoral, and the citizen powers.

The executive power is made up of the president and the cabinet. The president is elected to a five-year term and can be reelected to a second term. Cabinet members are appointed by the president, as is the vice president, who helps create new laws and policies.

The legislative power is unicameral, that is, only one group of people, the National Assembly, votes on the laws. Prior to the 1999 Constitution it was bicameral, meaning that a senate also had to vote on laws before they were passed, but the new Constitution did away with the senate. The National Assembly has 165 members, elected from all parts of the country, and 3 members of the assembly must belong to indigenous groups.

The Supreme Tribunal of Justice is the main body of the judicial power. The National Assembly elects its member judges for twelve-year terms. There are several layers of local courts and the Supreme Tribunal is the final court of appeal. Trials in Venezuela are resolved during hearings before a judge and jury.

The electoral branch is separate from all other branches of government. Its members are responsible for making sure election laws are followed.

The citizen power is sometimes called the moral branch, as it is in place to oversee that public ethics and morals are upheld, and to penalize those who don't comply. This group, called the Republican Moral Council, also makes sure that public money is used properly.

NATIONAL GOVERNMENT OF VENEZUELA

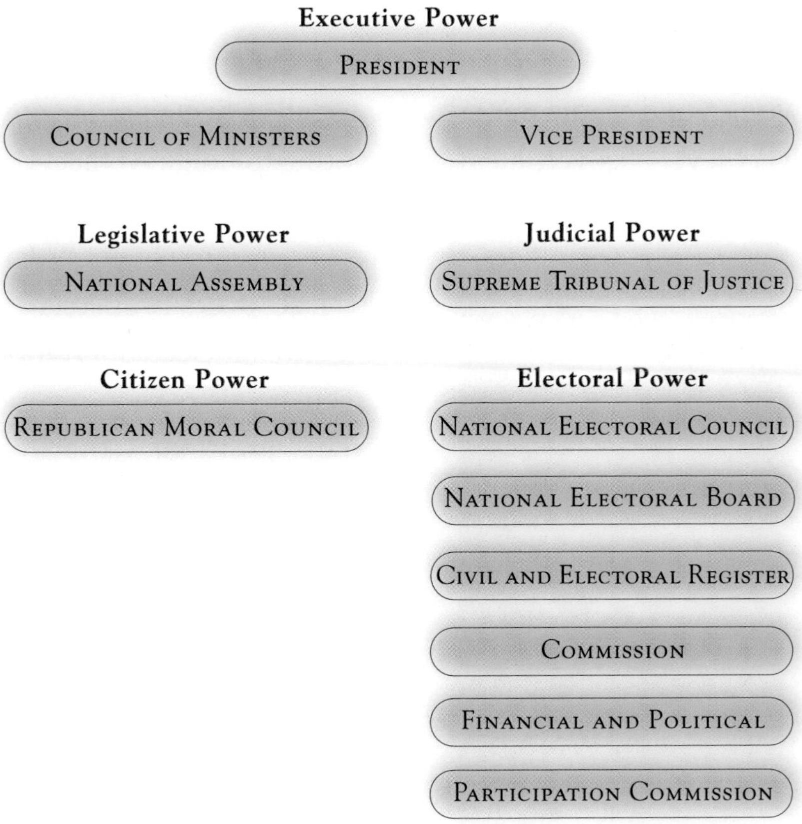

Executive Power

PRESIDENT

COUNCIL OF MINISTERS   VICE PRESIDENT

Legislative Power   **Judicial Power**

NATIONAL ASSEMBLY   SUPREME TRIBUNAL OF JUSTICE

Citizen Power   **Electoral Power**

REPUBLICAN MORAL COUNCIL   NATIONAL ELECTORAL COUNCIL

NATIONAL ELECTORAL BOARD

CIVIL AND ELECTORAL REGISTER

COMMISSION

FINANCIAL AND POLITICAL

PARTICIPATION COMMISSION

State and Local Governments

Venezuela is divided into twenty-two states, along with one federal district, and one federal dependency, made up of seventy-two island groups. Voters from each state elect governors to four-year terms. Each may be reelected for one additional consecutive term. Each state also has a Legislative Council with seven to fifteen members. They are elected to four-year terms and can be reelected twice.

The states are broken down into districts. Mayors, elected to four-year terms, as well as municipal councils lead these.

Minorities in Politics

Women and ethnic minorities have full rights to participate in every level of government, from voting to holding office. Both groups are well represented in local government, but in national elected offices they are underrepresented. Women hold just over 10 percent of the national elected positions. Women are also rare in top ministerial positions that are appointed by the president.

Just as Venezuelans spent decades fighting for independence, they are likely to continue working to put in place a government that finally meets their needs, providing stability, freedom, and economic security.

Irene Saez, mayor of the municipality of Chacao

Simón Bolívar

Nearly every city and village in the country has a plaza, or at least a statue, in his honor. The nation's currency is even named for him. No figure is more revered in Venezuela than Simón Bolívar.

Bolívar was born in Caracas on July 24, 1783. He inherited a great fortune from his parents when they died during his childhood. He spent most of this money trying to achieve his lifelong dream of freedom and unity for South America.

As a youngster, he was educated by private tutors, and later he traveled throughout Europe. He returned to Venezuela in 1810 to join in the revolt against Spain. He fought for the next two decades to rid South America of Spanish control, hoping to unite the countries into one strong republic. He commanded troops in Venezuela, Colombia, Ecuador, Peru, Panama, and Bolivia leading them all to victory.

Bolívar deserved the love and respect he received from people throughout much of South America. However, that was not enough to enable him to achieve his goal of unity. Though the republic of Gran Colombia united Venezuela, Colombia, and Ecuador for a time, it rapidly dissolved. Each nation had its own interests and problems and it was impossible for them to work together.

Even after the republic of Gran Colombia came apart in 1830, Bolívar refused to give up his dream. Though he resigned as president, he continued to urge the nations to unite. Many leaders turned against Bolívar, and soon the public did, too. Bolívar was brokenhearted, and his health grew terrible. He planned to leave South America for good, but never made it to Europe. He died in 1830, without money or friends, near the Colombian coast.

It took several decades, but eventually the people of South America, particularly Venezuela, realized the important, special role Bolívar had played in their history. Today, he is greatly beloved throughout the land and known as *El Libertador*, the Liberator.

Caracas: Did You Know This?

Caracas is the capital of Venezuela, a bustling, modern city still growing in the shadow of the nearby Andes. The city was named for the Indian tribe, the Caracas, that lived nearby when the city was founded in 1567.

Today, Caracas is home to almost 2 million Venezuelans. Many wealthy people live on large estates in the city, while poor people live in shacks built up the city's steep hillsides. Middle-class citizens fill the

city's thousands of apartment homes. Some residents have lived in the city all their lives, while others have recently arrived. All hope that Caracas will give them a chance at a good life, but that was more likely in the past. Caracas had a booming economy in the 1970s and 1980s, when oil was bringing a good price. When the oil prices fell, so did the city's economy. Today, there is an abundance of poverty and crowding in Caracas, but much good as well.

Plaza Bolívar is the center of the city where the liberator of Venezuela, Simón Bolívar, is honored with a statue. The plaza is a hub of activity, surrounded by many important government buildings including the *Capitolio Nacional*, where the Congress meets, and the *Casa Amarilla*, home to Venezuela's foreign ministry. Here also is the *Catedral*, the Catholic cathedral that houses the Bolívar family chapel. Bolívar's remains are kept at the Pantéon Nacional, or National Pantheon.

Caracas is the center for fine arts in Venezuela. Many of the buildings surrounding Plaza Bolívar contain great works of art, and there are outstanding history and art museums in the city as well. The national theater company, national symphony orchestra, and contemporary dance troupe are based here, all performing in the *Teatro Teresa Carreño*.

Population: 1,822,465

Year of Founding: 1567, by Diego de Losada

Average Daily Temperature: In January, 65°F (18°C); in July, 69°F (21°C)

Average Annual Rainfall: 33 inches (840 mm)

Altitude: 3,000 feet (914 m) above sea level

Caracas

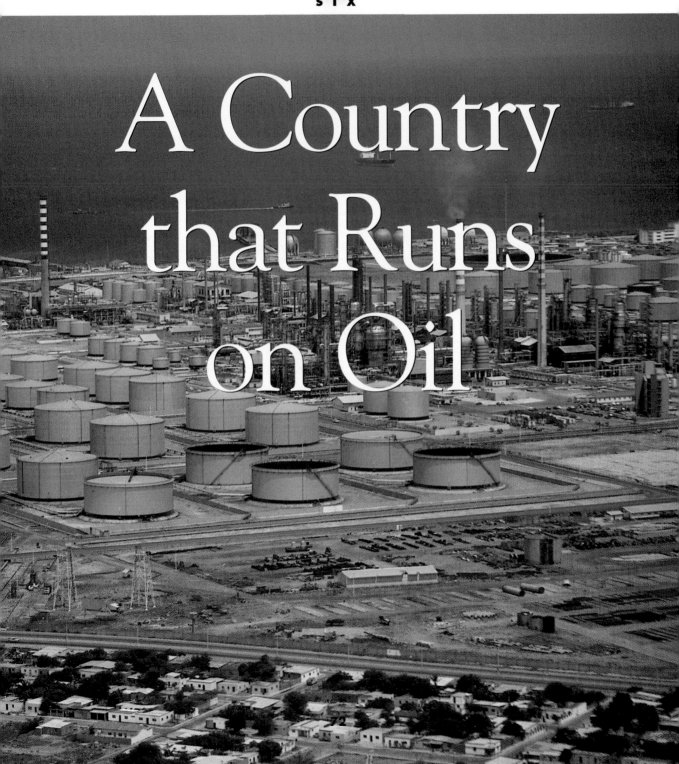

A Country that Runs on Oil

OIL IS THE BLOOD OF VENEZUELA'S ECONOMY. WHEN blood is rich with nutrients, the body it serves is healthy. When the blood is poor, so is the health. That's just how it is with oil in Venezuela. When the price of oil is good, when it's "rich," then the country's economy is usually healthy. When the price of oil is weak, however, so is Venezuela's economy.

Venezuela boomed when oil prices were high during the mid-1970s into the 1980s. Many fortunes were made by people in the oil industry. Money was pumped into the country's schools, hospitals, roads, and other public works projects. Hundreds of jobs were created. Venezuela had the highest income per person in South America. Times were good. In 1983 oil prices crashed and Venezuela's economy took a downturn. Fewer people were wealthy, and the government had less money to spend on its citizens.

When the hard times hit, Venezuelans realized just how dependent their country had been on oil. So much focus had been put on the petroleum industry that other industries were left to decay. Nearly all the country's food was imported, since

Opposite: **An oil refinery on the coast at Punto Fijo**

In a healthy economy modern malls in Caracas are busy with shoppers.

A large percent of Venezuelans live at or below poverty level.

agriculture was neglected. Manufacturing, long ignored, brought in little income. In just a few decades Venezuela went from being the wealthiest nation in South America to one of its poorest. More than 67 percent of its citizens live below the poverty level and nearly 70 percent of those are considered to be living in extreme poverty.

Venezuela is a nation blessed with many natural resources. There are other things people in Venezuela can do to build their economy. For now, though, oil is still the main focus of the nation's economy.

Oil and the Government

Venezuela's economy is dependent upon the price of oil because it is one of the country's greatest natural resources. Underneath the beautiful Venezuelan landscape is a vast supply of energy reserves—petroleum and gas. These are found primarily in the Maracaibo Basin as well as in the eastern part of the country. Venezuela has one of the world's largest supplies of hydrocarbons. It also has great hydroelectric resources, leading many to consider Venezuela as one of the most important energy sources in the Western Hemisphere. It is a founding member of OPEC (Organization of Petroleum Exporting Countries) and its third largest producer of oil.

The Guri Dam in Venezuela is South America's second largest hydroelectric plant.

Crude oil and refined oil are the main petroleum products in Venezuela, together providing nearly half of the nation's income in 2000. The country also is a major producer of natural gas and bitumen to make the liquid coal used in power plants.

Petroleos de Venezuela is the name of the country's oil monopoly owned and run by the government. Since it controls oil production, the government has a good deal of influence over many aspects of the economy. In recent years many economists believe this influence has not always been used wisely. Instead, politicians have made economic choices that will improve their personal situations rather than better the country over the long term.

The nation has shifted toward a growing dependence on the national oil company. In the meantime, other industries shrank as the government invested less in them.

Venezuelans shop at a discount market to cope with soaring prices.

Economic Problems

Today, the government's level of control over Petroleos de Venezuela has been weakening. In late 2002 employees of this company went on strike, seeking to force the president to resign, and to hold early elections. Chavez sent in military troops to take over oil production facilities. Venezuela faces other economic problems as well. The nation's tax authority reported that, in 2001, about 50 banks and 1,000 businesses in the country had evaded taxes for a loss of about $800 million in revenue for the government.

Inflation, or increasing costs for goods and services, is rising in Venezuela, too. Venezuela has the second highest rate of inflation in all of South America, while for the decade 1990 to 2000 the country's rate of economic growth was the lowest in South America.

For now, Venezuela's government and its economy are entwined with the oil industry. The country will need to build upon its other resources in order to improve its economy.

World Trade

Venezuela's location on the globe puts it in a good position to do business with much of the world. Venezuela is part of Latin America, so it has a handle on those markets, but it is very similar to the Caribbean nations, due to its long Caribbean coastline. The coastline gives it a low-cost way to do trading by sea. Venezuela is close to North America, and not too far from Europe, either. The United States is Venezuela's main trading partner, but Colombia, Brazil, Italy, Japan, Canada, and Germany are also important.

Ports along Venezuela's coast are busy trading hubs with many nations.

Coffee plantation

A cattle drive on the llanos

Agriculture has long been a part of Venezuela's economic history. The country has an ability to grow a wide variety of crops, since there is such diversity in the landscape. Its main crop is sugarcane, followed by tropical fruits such as bananas and oranges. Also important is maize, or corn, rice, cassava (a sort of potato), and coffee. Livestock is raised mainly in the llanos. Here ranchers raise some 15 million head of cattle, more than 3 million each of hogs and goats, and more than 1 million sheep. Poultry number more than 100 million.

What Venezuela Grows, Makes, and Mines

Agriculture (1999 est.)

Sugarcane	7.1 million metric tons
Tropical fruit	2.8 million metric tons
Maize	1 million metric tons

Manufacturing

Refined petroleum & petroleum products (2001 est.)	475 million barrels
Fertilizers (1998 est.)	806,000 metric tons
Aluminum (1999 est.)	570,000 metric tons

Mining

Petroleum (2001 est.)	1.2 billion barrels
Iron ore (1999 est.)	20 million metric tons
Bauxite (2001 est.)	5 million metric tons

Many of these agricultural products are exported to Venezuelan trading partners around the world.

Fishing

With its 1,736 miles (2,816 km) of Caribbean coastline it is no surprise that Venezuela has a strong fishing industry. Commercial fishing is based mainly in the east. There, sardines, shrimps, clams, mussels, and crabs are taken from the sea. Tuna fleets abound and take the fish to tuna canneries on the mainland for processing. Pearl fisheries are located near Margarita Island.

Forestry

Much of the Andes region is covered with trees. The Guayana region, too, looks like a carpet of leafy green trees when viewed

Weights and Measures

Venezuela uses the metric system of weights and measures. In the metric system, units of distance are based on the meter, weight is based on the gram, and volume is based on the liter.

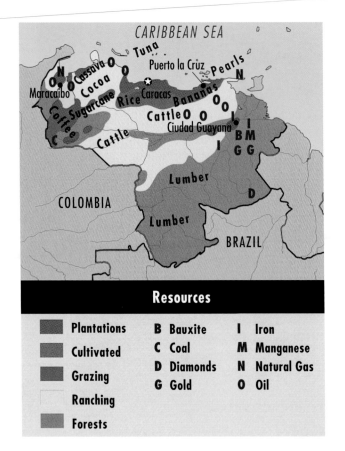

CARIBBEAN SEA

Tuna

Puerto la Cruz

Pearls

Maracaibo
Cassava
Cocoa

Coffee
Sugarcane
Rice
Caracas
Bananas

Cattle

Cattle
Ciudad Guayana

N
B M
G G

I

Lumber

D

COLOMBIA

Lumber

BRAZIL

Resources

Plantations	
Cultivated	
Grazing	
Ranching	
Forests	

B Bauxite
C Coal
D Diamonds
G Gold

I Iron
M Manganese
N Natural Gas
O Oil

from the sky. Still, Venezuela's forestry industry is very limited. It is simply too difficult to get to the trees. Few roads have been built into the Andes or the Guayana regions, and it would be very expensive to build roads that were adequate for forestry needs.

Some lumber is cut in more accessible parts of the country, though. It is used for building homes and furniture as well as for fuel and paper.

Mining and Manufacturing

Near the Orinoco River major amounts of iron ore have been mined since the deposits were found in the 1940s. Other minerals that have been mined in Venezuela include bauxite, diamonds, platinum, gold and silver, tin, copper, and salt.

Iron ore mine

The center of manufacturing in Venezuela is in Ciudad Guayana. It is in an area rich with natural resources, and located along the Orinoco River near enough to the sea for oceangoing ships to reach it. Steel and aluminum are among the major products manufactured in Venezuela, as well as construction materials, fertilizers, textiles, and processed foods. Many vehicles are assembled at plants there.

Currency: The Venezuelan Bolívar

When you consider that the basic unit of money in Venezuela is called the bolívar, after the great leader Simón Bolívar, it is no surprise that his face shows up on much of the currency (pictured). Not all banknotes carry his picture. Other people and things are pictured as well. In fact, many different things are seen on Venezuela's currency, for the bolívar notes are frequently changed.

Among them is Andrés Bello, who lived from 1781 to 1865. He was an important scholar and author in Venezuela. Another is José Antonio Páez, who lived from 1790 to 1873 and fought along with Bolívar against Spain. He was the first president of Venezuela. The intellectual Simón Rodríguez, who tutored Bolívar, is also depicted on some notes. He lived from 1771 to 1854.

Angel Falls is a natural scene shown on some notes. Colorful birds and flowers are also depicted in a nod to the country's rich supply of wildlife.

On some notes, important buildings in Venezuela's capital of Caracas are pictured. One of these is the Panteón Nacional, the mausoleum that holds the remains of several of Venezuela's great heroes, including most importantly, Bolívar's remains. Also depicted on currency are various images from the country's history, showing scenes from the country's struggle for independence.

Bolívares are divided into 100 céntimos, and there are coins for 25 and 50 céntimos, as well as for 1, 2, and 5 bolívares. These coins have little value, though, and most people don't carry them. Instead, they use the paper currency. This come in notes of 5, 10, 20, 50, 100, 500, 1,000, 2,000, 5,000, 10,000, and 20,000 bolívares.

The value of the bolívar is constantly changing. As of October 2001: US$1 = 773.8 bolívares, and in June 2002 US$1 = 135.6 bolívares.

With most government money being routed into the petroleum industry, manufacturing in Venezuela has not done well. With the many natural resources available in the country, much more manufacturing could take place, providing jobs and income. It will take money from foreign investors to increase manufacturing. The Venezuelan government officially welcomes foreign investment, but few outsiders are willing to invest money in a country that is so unstable. Foreign investment in the country is decreasing quickly.

Tourism

Venezuela, with its great diversity of landscapes, offers many delights to tourists. Those who enjoy deep-sea fishing for such trophies as barracuda, yellowfin tuna, and white and blue marlin will find great opportunities off the coast. Scuba divers, too, have found Venezuela's coast to be one of the best diving spots in the world with many types of corals and fish to view. People who would rather just laze in the sun on a white sand beach beneath a palm tree can do that, too. Guides take adventurous trekkers on journeys through the mountains and through the Gran Sabana as well. Both of these remote areas offer terrific terrain for those who like climbing, as well as great views as rewards for their hard work! Birdwatchers can find plenty to see in the skies above the llanos and in the rain forests. The array of exciting vacation opportunities in Venezuela is truly breathtaking.

Venezuelans are working to make the most of these opportunities. They are building hotels and resorts along the coast and establishing tourist camps in the more remote areas of the country. Guides to take adventure travelers into remote areas are building businesses. Tourism has the potential to be a main resource in Venezuela's economy in the coming years.

Tourists enjoy a tour of the Orinoco River

The People of Venezuela

T HE PEOPLE OF VENEZUELA ARE TALKATIVE, INFORMAL, AND open with their thoughts. They are affectionate and generous, even to people they've just met. They rarely put any long-lasting importance on friendships. They are funny and love to laugh, but avoid serious conversations. These are just some of the stereotypes of Venezuelans.

It would be a mistake to describe all the people in any country in a single way, to stereotype them. In any group there will be many people who do not fit the description. But there are cultural norms and values that are common to many people of any nation. These stereotypes do describe a majority of Venezuelans, especially the city dwellers. Venezuelans maintain a personality all their own.

Opposite: **Friendly faces of Venezuela**

Venezuelans are known to be colorful and cheerful people.

Friendly People

Venezuelans are usually expressive in their communication. They will wave their arms in seeming anger, but then quickly they will be laughing cheerfully. Venezuelans take great pride in their country, in their families, and in their work. Many also are very concerned with their appearance and go to great lengths to dress and look their best. They are also quite hospitable and it is important for them to

treat guests in their homes with as much extravagance as is possible. In many cases, they may only be able to offer a small snack and a cool drink, but it is provided graciously.

Outsiders sometimes have trouble with the fact that many Venezuelans seem to have little regard for time. They will often be up to an hour late for appointments. This is simply their more relaxed approach toward time. After a while those outsiders who were at first frustrated often find themselves adopting the easygoing attitude. Venezuelans are laid-back, but not lazy. Many work very hard to move ahead in life.

National pride is strong throughout the country. Venezuelans have survived many struggles, both throughout their history and in recent decades, too. It is no surprise that

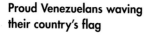

Proud Venezuelans waving their country's flag

people take great comfort in their flag and national anthem. These are some of the symbols that draw them together, along with great reverence for their hero, Simón Bolívar. They are proud that they have established and maintained their independence. Even though much of their current culture—fashion, sports, celebrities—is drawn from Europe and the United States, Venezuelans do not view this as a rejection of their own culture. Rather, they see these outside influences as evidence that Venezuela is an equal player in the modern world.

Population of the Major Cities of Venezuela	
Caracas	1,822,465
Maracaibo	1,207,513
Valencia	903,706
Barquisimeto	602,450
Ciudad Guayana	536,506

Population Statistics

Venezuela's population is mostly urban and young. Cities are home to 87 percent of its 23.9 million citizens—it is one of the most urbanized nations in all of Latin America. Children under

A crowded street in downtown Maracaibo

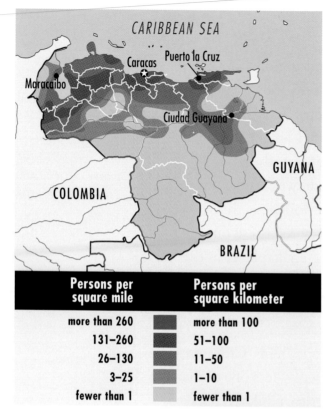

Persons per
square mile

Persons per
square kilometer

more than 260		more than 100
131–260		51–100
26–130		11–50
3–25		1–10
fewer than 1		fewer than 1

age fifteen make up one-third of the population, and 65 percent are under thirty. The country has a high birth rate and is growing rapidly. The population is predicted to grow to 29 million by the year 2010 and to double every thirty-three years. Most of the people who live in Venezuela are immigrants or descended from immigrants.

The largest ethnic group in Venezuela is known as *mestizo*, those who are a mixture of European, indigenous, and African backgrounds. They represent 69 percent of the population. Another 20 percent are white,

A mestizo man

while 9 percent are black of African descent. Some Venezuelans have had ancestors in the country for several hundred years or more. Others are fairly new arrivals. When the oil boom began in the 1920s, many people came from Spain, Italy, and Portugal to work and invest in the oil fields. Later, people arrived from Argentina, Chile, Uruguay, Colombia, Ecuador, and Peru. They came to escape the harsh economic and political conditions in their own countries.

Just 2 percent of the population are indigenous. They are isolated from the rest of the population in the nation's rural areas. They live in remote villages, mostly in the Orinoco Delta. While they are hanging on to their culture and traditions, it becomes increasingly difficult as tourism encroaches upon their lives. Though they are the country's true natives, they are nearly forgotten by society and government alike.

Ethnic Breakdown of the National Population

Mestizo (mixture of indigenous, African, and European origin)	69%
Whites of European descent	20%
Blacks of African descent	9%
Indigenous	2%

Indigenous Indians

There were tribes of indigenous people living throughout South America for thousands of years. When colonists arrived in the late 1400s and early 1500s they found large, well-organized tribes in parts of Mexico and Peru. These Indians, especially the Incas and the Aztecs, had great scientific knowledge with vibrant cultures, strong religions, and established communities.

Most indigenous people in Venezuela, however, lived in small tribes. Some were mostly hunters and gatherers, searching the wilderness for the resources they needed. Some were nomadic, meaning they moved from place to place in search

The Yanomamis

The Yanomamis are aborigines, the first inhabitants, of some 30,000 square miles (77,700 sq km) of dense rain forest in southern Venezuela and northern Brazil. Of all the indigenous people in Venezuela, this is the only group that has been able to avoid much modern influence. They have little contact with outsiders. They support themselves today as they have for centuries by growing food, gathering wild fruits, nuts, and vegetables from the surrounding rain forest, hunting for meat, and fishing. Their close community groups move together every few years when the resources become slimmer, relocating to a new area.

Entire communities of Yanomami people live together in large structures called *malocas*. These are circular buildings that are covered with thatch around the outside and open to the sky toward the center. Families each have separate areas within the malocas, which sometimes house more than 100 people. They cook their own meals around their own fires, but enjoy the closeness of the community.

The Yanomami have their own religious beliefs and practices. Shamans are their religious leaders who are responsible for getting rid of evil spirits within the community or within sick individuals. They use leaves and other items from nature that are believed to have special powers. These concoctions are often successful, for scientists have found that many jungle plants work as medicines.

When a member of the tribe dies the body is cremated and bones are ground and blended into a special mixture. Yanomami people believe that by drinking this, they can keep the spirit of the dead person with them.

Though the Venezuelan government has agreed to set aside a large piece of land for them in the state of Amazonas, where no outside development will be allowed, this has not yet happened. Instead, the land on which they live has been invaded by such people as gold miners, loggers, and cattle ranchers who want to make money using the resources there. Sometimes these outsiders carry with them diseases that the Yanomami people are unable to fight naturally. This has been happening for centuries. When Europeans first arrived in South America they brought smallpox, which killed thousands of indigenous people. As recently as 1998 the Yanomami people were exposed to yellow fever carried by outsiders who invaded their land. Many died.

of food. Others had basic farming skills, growing plants and raising the animals they needed.

When the Spanish colonists arrived and began to spread throughout South America, many indigenous Indians died. Some died because they were treated harshly by the colonists who made them slaves. More died from the diseases the Spaniards brought with them. The Indians had no natural immunities to such illnesses, especially smallpox. Still more died when they were forced onto new lands by the colonists and were unable to find the resources that they needed. At the time the Spaniards first arrived, about forty or fifty different tribes inhabited the land that is now Venezuela, but within 100 years, half had been wiped out.

Many Indians remained though, and the races began to mix. The early Spanish colonists did not bring women with them on the long, difficult journey. When it came time for them to marry, they took Indian women as brides. Their children became the first in Venezuela's large group of mestizos, or people of mixed racial heritage.

Black slaves were brought to Venezuela shortly after it became colonized to work on the plantations. Some were from Africa, while others came from the West Indies. These blacks also mixed with the Spaniards.

Because they have such a diverse mixture of origins in their history, there are no defining Venezuelan physical characteristics. Hair color, skin tone, and facial features come in all varieties. With their mixed ancestry and variety of looks, Venezuelans are fond of saying that theirs is a country without racism. To a large extent, this is true. Socially, people are not separated by color, but financially, they are. Most of the country's wealthiest people are white; its poorest are black. Economic differences keep people apart.

Language

Venezuela's national language is Spanish, one of the most commonly spoken languages in the world. The remote native

Advertising signs in Spanish

tribes have their own languages, most of which are still spoken. There are about thirty of these languages, which fall into three main categories: Arawak, Cariban, and Chibcha.

Most Venezuelans have learned a bit of English, but only basic terms. Few know enough to hold a full conversation unless they have studied English extensively, work in the travel industry, or have lived in the United States or another English-speaking nation for some time. People visiting Venezuela are well advised to learn enough Spanish to carry them in conversation if they want to be able to speak with the general public. Happily, they'll usually find that Venezuelans are patient, and more than willing to accommodate them in trying to communicate.

Though it is the same Spanish language that is spoken in so many parts of the world, Venezuelan Spanish does take on a few twists of its own. A few words have been added to the vocabulary—words that mostly shine a light on Venezuelan good humor and affection for others. *Vaya* shows admiration, while *zamo* is a teenage slang term for friend.

Some terms are versions of words from other languages, including English. *Rosbif* is roast beef, *fútbol* is soccer, and *chort* is a pair of shorts. Several English words, such as picnic, blue jean, fashion, and hobby, mean the same thing in Venezuela.

Body Language

The expression and sincerity that Venezuelans appreciate in their speech typically spill over into their body language as well. In general, they tend to stand very near the person with whom they're speaking, giving outsiders the feeling that their

Common Phrases	
¡Hola!	Hello!
Buenos días	Good day
Buenas noches	Good night
Adiós	Good-bye
Sí	Yes
No	No
Por favor	Please
Gracias	Thank you
De nada	You're welcome
Lo siento	I'm sorry
¿Cómo se llama usted?	What is your name?
¿Cómo estás?	How are you? (Familiar)
¿ Cómo está usted?	How are you? (Formal)
Señor/Señora/Señorita	Mr./Mrs./Miss
Hoy	Today
Mañana	Tomorrow
Ayer	Yesterday

Formal Names

Formal names in Venezuela are long, often with four or five parts. Venezuelans usually have two first names, similar to the first name and middle name, but they are more likely to use either one, though not necessarily at the same time. It can be confusing. The third name is typically the surname passed down from the father. The fourth name is the surname from the mother's family, and it is sometimes dropped. When a woman marries, she takes her husband's paternal surname, preceded by "de." This then replaces the maternal surname in her name.

Most first names are colorful, some with special meanings. Many times, two names are put together to make one, or children are given English names with Spanish spellings. The popular name *Esperanza* means hope, while another common name, *Mercedes*, means favor or gift.

personal space is being violated. This is just the Venezuelan way of showing interest and concern, along with looking intently into another's eyes, and hugging and kissing upon greeting friends.

Names

As in many other aspects of their life and speech, Venezuelans are informal when it comes to names, and will often use nicknames. Sometimes these are intimate and loving, though they may not seem so, such as when a woman calls her husband *gordito*, or fatty. Other times, nicknames will be used when the speaker doesn't know another's name. Then, a title will be quickly given, based on height, weight, hair or skin color, or some other physical attribute. These are not meant to be rude, rather, they are just straightforward and a simple way of discussing someone.

CHAPTER

EIGHT

Faith and
Spirituality

96

NEARLY ALL VENEZUELANS—96 PERCENT—ARE ROMAN Catholic. Another 2 percent are Protestant. The remaining 2 percent include Jews, Muslims, some native Indians who follow their own traditional religions (though most have been converted to Catholicism), and members of small cult religions.

Catholicism is not the official religion. The government does not force anyone to follow it. Its large following comes from a long history in the country, beginning with missionaries dating back to the early 1500s. The then-pope demanded that when the lands discovered by Columbus were conquered, the Indians must be converted to Christianity.

Opposite: **Though not the official religion, most Venezuelans practice Catholicism.**

Major Religions

Roman Catholics	96%
Protestants	2%
Other (Muslims, Jews, cult members, native religions)	2%

Structure of the Catholic Church

The Catholic Church, with more than 1 billion followers worldwide, has more members than does any other single Christian faith. As Christians, they believe that God entered the world through the birth of his son, Jesus, to Mary. Jesus's life and teachings, found in the New Testament of the Bible, form the basis of Catholic beliefs.

The church is structured with neighborhood parishes, each led by a priest at its base. These are organized into regional dioceses, with bishops at the head. The major church in each diocese is called a cathedral. Several dioceses combine in large groups to form archdioceses, led by archbishops.

The mass is the central rite of worship. It is celebrated daily in churches, and Catholics are expected to attend each Sunday and on several special church holidays throughout the year.

Catholics are different from many other Christians in their veneration, or worship, of saints. Catholics believe that when they pray to saints, the saints will take the prayers directly to God. The feast days of many saints are celebrated throughout the year. These feast days are important in Venezuela, where villages often stage flamboyant festivals on their patron saints' feast days.

Catholics attend mass during Holy Week in Caracas

Religious Festivities in Venezuela

Since nearly all of Venezuela's residents are Catholics or Protestants, Christian holidays are widely observed, including Holy Week, prior to Easter. Even though Christmas and Easter are major religious events, the Venezuelan love for a good party shines through. The festivities are not only religious in nature. There are parades with lots of dancing, music, and good food. Feast days of saints are noted, too. Many communities and parishes have specific patron saints whom they honor with grand celebrations on their feast days.

Catholic History in Venezuela

Catholicism had a strong influence in the development of European culture. As Europeans spread their culture throughout much of the world during the colonial period, the Catholic faith spread as well. Spaniards, in particular, were eager to bring church teachings to each region they conquered. Venezuela was no different.

The first attempt at conversion in Venezuela was a failure. Franciscan and Dominican friars, members of Catholic brotherhoods, were sent from Spain to Venezuela in 1513. They went to Cumaná, and were quickly slaughtered by the locals, an act of revenge for all the atrocities the Indians had suffered at the hands of early explorers who sacked their villages.

The Píritu Indians welcomed the first successful missions into Venezuela in 1650. In the land that is now the northern state of Anzoátegui, friars were able to set up small communities called *pueblos de indios*, or Indian towns. Sometimes Indians were attracted to these settlements by gifts; other times

This statue commemorates the meeting of Spanish friars and local Indians.

they were captured and forced to live there. Once there, they were lectured repeatedly by the missionaries on the wrongs of their native religions and the sins they were committing against Christianity. Eventually most Indians broke down and converted. They provided the labor for the town and were allowed to keep half of their profits, while the rest of the profits went to the missionaries and the king of Spain.

Eventually more missionaries arrived and settled similar pueblos de indios throughout Venezuela. A large concentration was located near Caracas. These communities brought some organization to Venezuelan society, though much of the native culture was lost. It is because of these communities that Venezuela is a Spanish-speaking, mostly Catholic, nation to this day.

By the early 1800s the Catholic religion was a major part of Venezuelan society. The archdiocese of Caracas had been established, and churches were the centers of society in cities and villages throughout the country. In 1820 there were 640 priests in Venezuela. Then, heavy-handed political regimes took control of the country. They saw the church as their opposition, and established laws to weaken it. Many of the routines of life, from birth to marriage to death, had once been accompanied by religious ceremonies. The government worked to make these secular, or without religion. Religious symbols were removed from cemeteries. Seminaries, where priests were trained, were closed. Property was taken away from religious groups. By 1855 there were only 154 priests left in the country. More than half the parishes had been abandoned. Guzmán Blanco, who became president and dictator of

Venezuela in 1870, was perhaps the harshest. He forced the archbishop of Caracas out of the country and completely ended all ties to the Vatican. The government had succeeded in diminishing the role of the Catholic Church in Venezuela.

People did not stop being Catholic, though. Instead, they substituted informal religious practices, conducted within their families, in place of the formal religion that had been ousted from their country. The Catholic faith was passed down from generation to generation, mostly by mothers and grandmothers. Priests and other aspects of the official Catholic Church became less important. This form of religion took hold in Venezuela, and today it remains a strong practice.

By the early 1900s the Catholic Church began an effort to rebuild its position within Venezuelan society. Parishes were once again staffed with priests, and many Catholic schools were established. Today, the schools continue, and many have the specific mission to educate the country's poorest children.

Catholics Today

Though the numbers of Catholics remain high in Venezuela, the level of true devotion to the faith is dwindling. Only about 20 percent regularly attend Sunday mass in the country's beautiful churches. Some say that Venezuelans became more materialistic and less interested in religion during the wealthy days of the oil boom. However, there are other reasons why not all Venezuelan Catholics regularly attend mass.

Religious Holidays in Venezuela

Epihany	January 6
Holy Thursday	Spring
Good Friday	Spring
Easter	Spring
Ascension	Late spring
Corpus Christi	Early summer
Assumption	August 15
All Saints' Day	November 1
Immaculate Conception	December 8
Christmas Day	December 25

One problem is a lack of space. Most parishes in North America and Europe have about 2,500 to 5,000 people, on average. The average Venezuelan parish, however, has more than 20,000 members, far more than can fit into church for Sunday services.

Another reason for the lack of churchgoing has its roots in history. When the government ousted many of the country's priests, Catholics, out of necessity, turned toward more private religious ceremonies and practices within their families. Today, that tradition lives on. It is another reason that in a nation in which most citizens are Catholic, the percentage who attend church regularly is fairly small.

South America's largest mosque, Sheikh Ibrahim Mosque, Caracas

Other Religions

Members of other faiths are in a distinct minority in Venezuela, but they make their presence known. The percentage of Protestants is small, but growing. Many Protestant missionaries are at work in the barrios helping the poor and have been successful at converting many to Protestant faiths.

The largest mosque in South America is found in central Caracas. A beautiful building, it is a popular tourist attraction, but, more important, it is the central gathering place for Muslim worshippers.

Most of the nation's several thousand Jews live in Caracas and Maracaibo. They operate several schools and synagogues in those cities.

The Cult of Maria Lionza

Cults have attracted a small number of followers. Perhaps the largest cult group, and one of the strangest, surrounds the mythical Maria Lionza (below). This cult started in the hills near the small town of Chivacoa in the Andes, but it is has followers in all layers of Venezuelan society from the small rural villages to the modern city of Caracas. There, visitors to the city's central district are often stunned to see a statue of Maria Lionza, naked, riding on a tapir. Maria Lionza is the daughter of an Indian man and a Spanish Creole woman, supposedly a witch. In the legend, two henchmen usually accompany her, and together they are known as the *tres poderosos*, or "three powers." Maria Lionza is loved as the goddess of nature, one who protects Venezuela's environment. On the *Día de la Raza*, her worshippers come out in force. They gather on hillsides to create altars and shrines, and make offerings in her honor. Cult priests use charcoal to decorate their bodies, then fall into a trance, aided by drinking rum.

From Baseball to Ballet

104

SOCCER IS THE MOST POPULAR SPORT IN ALL OF SOUTH America, with one exception. In Venezuela, people go crazy for baseball. Venezuelans follow their local professional teams fervently, with thousands attending the games, waving banners and cheering wildly.

This is mostly due to influence from the United States. Americans who came to Venezuela to work during the early days of the oil boom brought the game with them. Over the years, it began to catch on among Venezuelans, particularly after professional winter league teams formed during the 1940s. This season runs through the winter months. During the summer months, when the local teams aren't active, fans follow American baseball, paying special attention to those players from Venezuela who have made it to *Las Grandes Ligas*, "The Big Leagues."

Basketball and bullfighting are two other popular spectator sports in Venezuela. Basketball, like baseball, is played in Venezuela during the time

Opposite: **Venezuelan little leaguers hope of making it to the big leagues one day.**

Locals play an informal game of basketball

Great Venezuelan Shortstops

Omar Vizquel (*above*), shortstop for the Cleveland Indians, is the winner of nine straight Golden Glove awards. This award is given each year to the best fielder in the National League and the American League. His talent has attracted the attention of his fellow citizens in Venezuela, where he has many fans. He was born on April 24, 1967, in Caracas, and became a Cleveland Indian in 1994. He has said that whenever he steps onto the field, he feels as if he is representing all of Venezuela.

Many consider shortstop Luis Aparicio (*right*) to be the greatest Venezuelan baseball player ever. Known to his fans as "Little Looie," he had an eighteen-year career with the major leagues, beginning in 1956. He, too, won nine Golden Glove awards during the late 1950s, 1960s, and 1970, while playing for the Chicago White Sox and the Baltimore Orioles. He capped off his career by being named to the Baseball Hall of Fame in Cooperstown, New York. Some of the records Aparicio broke as a shortstop are still in place today, including the all-time record for most games played at the shortstop position, 2,581.

when American teams are not playing. This enables many professional players from the United States to play on the eight Venezuelan teams, as well. Bullfighting takes place in bullrings throughout Venezuela. These feature great pageantry and elaborate costumes, similar to the Spanish bullfights that inspired them.

Soccer (fútbol), so popular elsewhere in South America, is largely ignored in Venezuela. Most fans get really crazy about soccer only during the World Cup, when the world champion team is decided.

Bullfights are a popular pastime in Venezuela.

Venezuelans enjoy watching sports, but they like participating in them as well. Sportfishing is popular in Venezuela. Some consider the waters off Venezuela to be the best fishing grounds in the world for many large fish, particularly blue and white marlin, yellowfin tuna, and swordfish. These fish can weigh up to 150 pounds (68 kg) and even bigger. Blue marlin often weigh as much as 350 pounds (159 kg). Other popular oceanfront activities include sailing, windsurfing, snorkeling, and scuba diving.

Hiking is popular here, and in recent years a favorite goal among hikers has been making it to the top of El Ávila, a

Windsurfing off Margarita Island

Bolas Criollas

Bolas Criollas is the Venezuelan version of bowling, and it's a very popular game, particularly among people living in the country's rural areas. It gives them a good opportunity to get together with friends and catch up on news while enjoying themselves.

Players form two teams of four members. They play on a bare dirt surface of any size they agree upon. Each team has several wooden balls, about the size of baseballs, that they throw at a target, which is another ball called a *mingo*. Each team tries to get as close to the mingo as possible. Spectators cheer on their favorite teams in this lively game.

mountain near Caracas. There are different trails for all ability levels, so many can participate, and it has become a social event for weekend crowds.

Music

Venezuelans love music. It blares from the buses, people hum and sing on the streets and in their homes, and cowboys cry out tunes while they ride through the llanos. Many types of music make up the background noise to life in Venezuela.

There is a diversity of sound, thanks to the many cultures that have come together to make up the nation. Some of the music is taken from the traditions of the Indians native to Venezuela. Spanish influences show up as well as African and Caribbean, with Western styles of music creeping in more and more. The rhythms are usually fast. Salsa music is frequently heard and is usually blaring in the streets, coming from city buses. Merengue is a similar type of dance tune, introduced to the country in the 1930s. Rumba, calypso, and reggae get Venezuelans moving, too. All these styles are Caribbean with a strong African influence.

Miss Universe

Beauty is big business in Venezuela. In a country where great attention is paid to appearance, it makes sense that beauty pageants are popular. Aspiring models, singers, actresses—they all know that winning the title Miss Venezuela almost certainly assures them of success in their careers. The actress María Conchita Alonso, who has performed in two dozen American films, got her start as a Miss Venezuela. It doesn't stop at Miss Venezuela, though. The nation has a great history of its representatives going on to become Miss Universe!

In fact, there is a special school in Caracas, the Miss Academy, where young women enroll to learn the secrets of winning beauty pageants. They gladly pay the hefty tuition to learn how to carry themselves onstage, perform during an interview, enhance their beauty, and increase their odds of wearing the crown. It works. Graduates of the academy include four Miss Universes, five Miss Worlds, and a host of runners-up.

Oscar d' León, loved by Venezuelans as the Devil of Salsa, has been popular for decades. Franco de Vita is another popular Venezuelan singer. He began recording in 1982, and he continues to produce successful recordings today with songs about love and social problems.

An Andean musical group performs in Caracas

Traditional folk music is one type of music that's popular in Venezuela, and several musical groups specialize in playing the different styles from regions throughout the country. Un Solo Pueblo, which means "one people," is one such group working to make sure that traditional music is not forgotten. They attract large crowds wherever they play.

The main instruments used in Venezuelan music are a small four-stringed guitar known as the *cuatro*, *maracas*, and drums to keep the fast, pounding beat that is so common. It is hard to sit still listening to Venezuelan music, and dancing is an important part of the music scene as well.

Devil dancers take to the streets on Corpus Christi Day.

Dance

Joropo, the country's national dance, began as a country dance for couples, though it has its origins in Spain. The word comes from the Arabic word *xarop*, which means syrup. There are variations of joropo in each region of Venezuela, but it is danced at nearly all festivals.

Another dance popular at festivals is the devil dance. On the Catholic holy day of Corpus Christi, the *diablos danzantes*, devil dancers, take to the streets in cities and towns throughout the country. They make loud noises and dance wildly wearing colorful clothing and fearsome masks. The dancers are members of special societies that make the religious promise to dance in return for a special favor from God. This tradition goes back to the fifth century in Europe and was brought to Venezuela by the conquistadors.

Professional dancing also has its place in Venezuelan culture. There are several outstanding ballet companies such as the Ballet Nacional de Caracas and the Ballet Contemporáneo, as well as such contemporary dance companies as Danzahoy and Contradanza.

Professional performers of the Ballet Metropolitaneo de Caracas

Birth, Marriage, and Death Customs

Just as much of the art and music of Venezuela have their roots in religion, so do the customs surrounding birth, marriage, and death. The rules of the Roman Catholic Church provide the structure for how these important events are acknowledged by Venezuelans, since most people in the country are Catholic.

Baptism makes a newborn a member of the Catholic Church, so it is important that babies be baptized soon after birth. A priest blesses the baby and sprinkles it with holy water, while parents and godparents, selected to help make sure the child is raised properly, promise to guide the child. It is a joyous celebration, and often, the large extended family will gather and bring gifts to the new baby and parents.

When a young Venezuelan man wishes to get married, he will usually ask the woman's father for his permission before proposing to his bride-to-be. Weddings are elaborate affairs. The church ceremony includes verses that the bride and groom sing to each other, promising to be faithful to one another for life. A grand celebration, with food, music, and dancing follows.

Even at death, large crowds of family and friends gather, once again, to mourn the loss of a loved one. People who barely even knew the deceased will come to the family to pay respects. During the funeral, the deceased person's soul will be committed to God in Heaven, where Catholic believers expect that he or she will live forever.

Museo de Arte Contemporáneo de Caracas Sofía Imber

Museo de Arte Contemporáneo de Caracas Sofía Imber, or the Sofía Imber Museum of Contemporary Art, is one of the finest art museums in South America. Located in Caracas, it contains the works of many prominent contemporary Venezuelan artists, including such painters as Carlos Cruz Dies, Jesús Soto, and Alejandro Otero, and such sculptors as Marisol. Marisol's "Woman and Dog" sculpture is pictured. This museum also houses works by famed artists from throughout the world, including a large collection of paintings by Pablo Picasso, as well as works by Matisse, Chagall, and Henry Moore.

Art

Venezuela's rich landscape and history of struggle have inspired many artists. Several great painters and sculptors from this background have come to become appreciated around the world. Among them are the painters Cristóbal Rojas and Arturo Michelena. Armando Reverón is another fine artist from Venezuela. Though he studied art in Spain and France, he was eager to return home. He depicted, in his own unique style, the country's land and seascapes in many of his works.

Venezuelan writer Rómulo Gallegos

Novelist Arturo Uslar Pietri

Literature

Venezuela has produced several outstanding authors. One of the most famous is Rómulo Gallegos who has written such novels as *Doña Bárbara*, *Canaima*, and *El Forastero*, with themes including civil war, man and his struggle with nature, and the power of the jungle. Another important writer is Arturo Uslar Pietri. He has written novels about Venezuela's history, and has helped to make history, too, as a politician and television commentator.

Daily Life

In the last forty years Venezuela went from being a poor, undeveloped agricultural nation, to one that was suddenly flooded with oil money. Cities grew, roads, schools, and hospitals were built, and people enjoyed great spending sprees. Then, just as quickly as the wealth arrived, it was gone. Now Venezuelans are left with the habits of a wealthy nation, trying to adjust to being poor again. These changes have taken place so rapidly that the country is left with traditional habits confronted with modern desires.

Opposite: **Daily life in busy Caracas is similar to that of other modern cities.**

Venezuelan women in Western style dress

Clothing

Traditional Venezuelan dress for men is the *liqui-liqui*, pants with a straight-collared jacket. It is usually white or cream-colored, and is constructed of lightweight cotton so that it's cool even on the hottest days. It is occasionally worn for special occasions and business events. A narrow-brimmed hat completes the look.

Traditional dresses for women are full-skirted and colorful, but rarely seen. They are worn only for traditional dances and other events, but never as other than a costume. Venezuelan women typically adopt a clothing style similar to what is seen in North America. Jeans and T-shirts are popular with children and teens; adults wear skirts or dresses for work and formal occasions.

In most situations, the clothing seen in Venezuela is not much different from what is worn in the warmer regions of the United States. It's a nation that likes to dress up, and great care is taken to look nice at all times. Shopping is a favorite pastime here, and even though the country is poor, the many stores selling clothing and other goods hide that fact.

Shopping is a popular way to spend an afternoon in Venezuela.

Housing

Housing is varied throughout the country. There are differences between how people live in the mountains and on the coast, in rural areas, and in the city. The most obvious difference between homes is dependent upon the wealth of its owner. Venezuela's many poor live in shanties, while middle-class people live in high-rise apartments, and the wealthy live in large homes.

The shanties, or barrios, are usually built onto the hillsides of the large cities, often right next to garbage dumps and filthy industrial sites. Some are built of corrugated steel, others of clay or cement. Each is typically no larger than one room. Neighborhoods in these districts often lack plumbing and electricity and usually have few services such as garbage disposal. Disease and crime are rampant. Most barrio dwellers came to Venezuela's big cities from the llanos and other poor regions of the country. They came looking for work.

Hillside barrios

Most Venezuelans live in rented apartments or flats. The middle class, made up of such people as small business owners, teachers, and government workers, live in the nicer high rises, while laborers live cramped in smaller apartments.

The large, often gated estates on the outskirts of town, called *quintas*, are reserved for the richest people in the country. These homes have an American or European flair, and beautiful

Middle class Venezuelans reside in new apartment houses like this one in Ciudad Guayana.

gardens, often with swimming pools. They have high security, too, often employing guards or keeping dogs on the grounds.

It's not uncommon for large, extended Venezuelan families to live together in the same home. Family is, after all, a very important part of the fabric of Venezuelan lives. Grandparents, aunts and uncles, and cousins may all coexist in one building, or they may live in a series of smaller homes built close together.

Food

Though Venezuela is a relatively poor country, it is rich in several natural resources, and one of its most bountiful resources is a great supply of food. The nation's cuisine is varied with a wide selection of fruits and vegetables, plenty of meat and seafood, and cooking influences from around the world. It's no wonder Venezuelans love to eat!

Arepa sandwich

The day begins with a hearty breakfast followed by a substantial lunch and a lighter dinner in the evening, interspersed with snacks throughout the day. At any of these meals it is likely that one thing served will be arepas.

Arepas are the main staple of Venezuelan cuisine. These are thick, flattened balls of fried or baked corn or wheat flour. The country's poor eat lots of them, but so do the wealthy—the difference lies in the fillings. Arepas can be filled with just about anything—meats, cheeses, jelly, or vegetables. Some favorite fillings include tuna or chicken salad, shredded beef, or ham and cheese. Octopus or baby shark are other options. Arepas usually accompany Venezuela's national dish, *pabellón criollo*.

A common breakfast would be an arepa or two, stuffed with scrambled eggs with onion and tomato, washed down with

Pabellón Criollo

Pabellón criollo, Venezuela's national dish, is a hearty, flavorful dish that includes a number of common Venezuelan foods. In it black beans are combined with shredded beef and seasoned with onions, garlic, green peppers, tomatoes, and cilantro. This is served atop a mound of rice alongside a fried egg and strips of fried plantain. White cheese is grated over the top. Pabellón is a typical meal in many working-class Venezuelan homes and is often served in restaurants as well.

There are slight variations to pabellón criollo in different parts of the country. Along the Caribbean coast, seafood sometimes replaces the shredded beef. In some places condiments such as Worcestershire sauce, or even ketchup or soy sauce, may be added to the mix.

plenty of coffee with milk, fruit juice, or hot chocolate. Lunch, the biggest meal of the day, is often large and indulgent. Venezuelans usually have two hours off during the workday, so many travel home for lunch. Some common entrées may be ham hocks, or steak, perhaps seafood for those along the coast. Beans are a typical side dish, as are rice, salads, or potatoes. Dinner in the evening is light. Sometimes it is a scaled-down version of lunch, at other times a simple arepa or two is fine.

Venezuela's bountiful selection of tropical fruits makes a fine and typical accompaniment to many meals. Oranges, pineapples, papayas, strawberries, passion fruit, watermelon, limes, and avocados are plentiful. Street vendors with these tasty treats are

A produce stand displays Venezuela's many tropical fruits.

Hallaca, the Christmas Treat

During the Christmas season Venezuelan cooks pull out all the stops to create a special dish, hallaca, served only during the holidays. This delicious food, eagerly awaited each year, is a packet of cornmeal dough, steamed in a wrapping of palm leaves and bound with string. Inside is a filling of pork, chicken, and beef, mixed with olives, capers, raisins, tomatoes, onion, garlic, and green pepper, sugar, cumin, black pepper, parsley, and almonds. These were first made by servants trying to use up leftovers from their master's table. It takes many hours, even days, to prepare this dish, which is why it is served only at one special time each year.

found in most cities. One unusual fruit is called mamones. This pink-fleshed fruit, about the size of a tennis ball, has a green rind. Venezuelans buy these for their delicious juice.

Few meals would be complete without dessert, for Venezuelans love their sweets. Cakes are favorites, especially carrot cake and a coconut cake known as *bienmesabe*. Fried dough sprinkled with sugar and cinnamon, called *churros*, is another popular treat.

Official National Holidays in Venezuela

New Year's Day	January 1
Holy Thursday	Spring
Good Friday	Spring
Declaration of Independence	April 19
Labor Day	May 1
Battle of Carabobo	June 24
Independence Day	July 5
Birth of Simón Bolívar	July 24
Civil Servants' Day	September 4
Discovery Day	October 12
Christmas Day	December 25

A happy pet owner shows off his parrot.

Pets

Though dogs are seen frequently in Venezuela, usually they are for security or are roaming wild. The thin and scruffy cats that are seen are almost always wild. Few Venezuelans would ever consider keeping such an animal as a pet. Animals in the home are considered unclean and a waste of money. The most common pets in the nation are probably parrots, kept in cages on the balconies in poor areas of cities.

Grade school students

Education

Schooling in Venezuela is much like it is in Canada and the United States. Children under six years old may attend classes called *preescolar*. After that, eleven grades of school are mandatory until age eighteen. Students must pass classes in all subject areas before they can move up to the next grade. There are several private schools for those who are able to afford them, and many Catholic schools offer scholarships, or reduced rates, for students with low incomes.

The best university in the country is Universidad Central in Caracas. Most Venezuelan universities are private, and only the top students are able to attend.

Those students who do go on to study at the university have a great challenge ahead of them. They are the teenagers of today who will go on to become the leaders of Venezuelan society, business, and government. They are the ones who can help Venezuela become the great nation that it has the potential to be.

High school seniors perform an experiment in chemistry class.

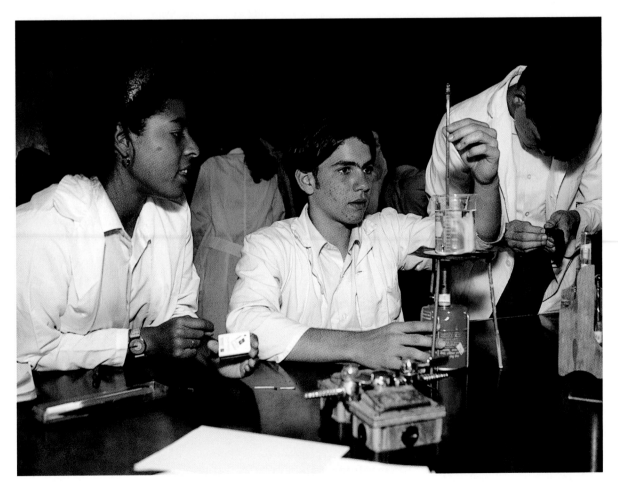

Timeline

Venezuelan History

First people arrive in Venezuela. **14,000** B.C.

Christopher Columbus becomes the first
European to visit Venezuela. A.D. **1498**

Venezuela gets its name, meaning "Little
Venice," from Amerigo Vespucci. **1499**

Franciscan and Dominican friars establish first
missions along Venezuelan coast. **1513**

Cumaná becomes the first Spanish town
settled in continental South America. **1521**

Caracas is founded. **1567**

Smallpox, introduced by Spaniards, wipes out
many native Venezuelan tribes. **1580**

Venezuela is first Spanish colony to declare its
independence, becoming what was then
known as the Republic of Gran Colombia. **1811**

Simón Bolívar is elected president of the
Republic of Gran Colombia. **1819**

World History

2500 B.C. Egyptians build the Pyramids
and the Sphinx in Giza.

563 B.C. The Buddha is born in India.

A.D. **313** The Roman emperor Constantine
recognizes Christianity.

610 The Prophet Muhammad begins preaching
a new religion called Islam.

1054 The Eastern (Orthodox) and Western
(Roman) Churches break apart.

1066 William the Conqueror defeats
the English in the Battle of Hastings.

1095 Pope Urban II proclaims the First Crusade.

1215 King John seals the Magna Carta.

1300s The Renaissance begins in Italy.

1347 The Black Death sweeps through Europe.

1453 Ottoman Turks capture Constantinople,
conquering the Byzantine Empire.

1492 Columbus arrives in North America.

1500s The Reformation leads to the birth
of Protestantism.

1776 The Declaration of Independence
is signed.

1789 The French Revolution begins.

Venezuelan History

Bolívar and his troops defeat the Spanish in the Battle of Carabobo. The Republic of Gran Colombia expands to unify Venezuela, Colombia, Ecuador, and Panama.	1821
Venezuela secedes from Gran Colombia and is established as a republic. José Antonio Páez becomes first president of Venezuela.	1830
Páez is exiled to New York City.	1850
Juan Vincente Gómez becomes a harsh dictator of Venezuela. He rules until 1935.	1908
Venezuela's oil boom begins with the drilling of a successful well near Lake Maracaibo.	1922
A citizens' political party, Acción Democrática, joined with the military to take control of the government.	1945
The military takes over the government following a bloodless coup.	1948
Civilian rule is reestablished. Rómulo Betancourt is president.	1959
A new Venezuelan Constitution is approved.	1961
The first time in Venezuela's history that the ruling party peacefully turned over power to its opposition.	1969
The government nationalizes the petroleum industry. Oil prices rise.	1976
Falling oil prices begin the decline of the Venezuelan economy.	1983
Military forces, led by Hugo Chávez, try to take control of government, but are defeated.	1992
Hugo Chávez becomes president. Floods and landslides kill thousands of Venezuelans.	1998
Venezuela gets a new Constitution and is formally renamed the Bolivarian Republic of Venezuela.	1999
Chávez is reelected.	2000
Coup attempt against Chávez fails.	2002
Protests and strike against Chavez continue.	2003

World History

1865	The American Civil War ends.
1914	World War I breaks out.
1917	The Bolshevik Revolution brings communism to Russia.
1929	Worldwide economic depression begins.
1939	World War II begins, following the German invasion of Poland.
1945	World War II ends.
1957	The Vietnam War starts.
1969	Humans land on the moon.
1975	The Vietnam War ends.
1979	Soviet Union invades Afghanistan.
1983	Drought and famine in Africa.
1989	The Berlin Wall is torn down, as communism crumbles in Eastern Europe.
1991	Soviet Union breaks into separate states.
1992	Bill Clinton is elected U.S. president.
2000	George W. Bush is elected U.S. president.
2001	Terrorists attack World Trade Towers, New York and the Pentagon, Washington, D.C.

Fast Facts

Official name: Bolivarian Republic of Venezuela

Capital: Caracas

Official language: Spanish

Caracas

Venezuela's flag

Scarlet macaw

Official religion:	None, though 96 percent of the population is Roman Catholic
Year of founding:	1811
National anthem:	"Gloria al Bravo Pueblo" ("Glory to the Brave People")
Government:	Federal republic
Chief of state:	President
Head of state:	President
Area and dimensions of country:	352,143 square miles (912,050 sq km)
Greatest distance north to south:	790 miles (1,271 km)
Greatest distance east to west:	925 miles (1,489 km)
Land and water borders:	The Caribbean Sea is to its north. To the west is Colombia, with Brazil to the south and Guyana to the east.
Highest elevation:	16,427 feet (5,007 m) at Pico Bolívar
Lowest elevation:	Sea level along the coastline
Highest average temperatures:	69°F (21°C) in Caracas; 85°F (29°C) in Maracaibo
Lowest average temperatures:	65°F (18°C) in Caracas: 81°F (27°C) in Maracaibo
Average annual precipitation:	33 inches (84 cm) in Caracas; 23 inches (58 cm) in Maracaibo

Angel Falls

Currency

National population:	23,916,810	
Population of largest cities:	Caracas	1,822,465
	Maracaibo	1,207,513
	Valencia	903,706
	Barquisimeto	602,450
	Ciudad Guayana	536,506

Famous landmarks:
- ▶ *World's Longest Cable Car*, Mérida
- ▶ *Angel Falls*, south of Ciudad Bolívar
- ▶ *Guri Dam*, on the Caroní River in the Gran Sabana
- ▶ *TeatroTeresa Carreño*, Caracas
- ▶ *Lake Maracaibo*, Maracaibo
- ▶ *Roraima Tepuis*, near the border with Brazil and Guyana

Industry: Petroleum, iron ore, cereals, fruit, sugar, and coffee

Currency: The Venezuelan bolívar. As of June 2002: US$1 = 135.6 bolívares. Its value fluctuates rapidly.

System of weights and measures: metric system

Common terms and phrases:

¡Hola!	Hello!
Buenos días	Good day
Buenas noches	Good night
Adiós	Good-bye
Sí	Yes
No	No
Por favor	Please

Schoolchildren

Simón Bolívar

Gracias	Thank you
De nada	You're welcome
Lo siento	I'm sorry
¿Cómo se llama usted?	What is your name?
¿Cómo estás? (Familiar)	How are you?
¿Cómo está usted? (Formal)	How are you?
Señor/Señora/Señorita	Mr./Mrs./Miss
Hoy	Today
Mañana	Tomorrow
Ayer	Yesterday

Famous Venezuelans:

Luis Aparicio   (1934–)
Baseball player

Rómulo Betancourt   (1908–1981)
Venezuelan president

Simón Bolívar   (1783–1830)
Venezuelan president and liberator

Hugo Chávez   (1954–)
Venezuelan president

Juan Vincente Gómez   (1864–1935)
Dictator

José Antonio Páez   (1790–1873)
First president of Venezuela

Omar Vizquel   (1967–)
Baseball player

To Find Out More

Nonfiction

▶ Baguley, Kitt. *Culture Shock! Venezuela*. Portland, OR: Graphic Arts Center Publishing, 2001.

▶ Baynham, Angela, ed. *Insight Guide: Venezuela*. London: Apa Publications, 2000.

▶ Morrison, Marion. *Venezuela*. Philadelphia: Chelsea House Publishers, 1999.

▶ Rawlins, Carol B. *The Orinoco River*. New York: Franklin Watts, 1999.

▶ Schwartz, David M. *Yanomami, People of the Amazon*. New York: Lothrop, Lee & Shepard, 1995.

▶ Sirimarco, Elizabeth. *Yanomamis*. Mankato, MN: Smart Apple Media, 2000.

▶ Winter, Jane Kohen. *Venezuela*. Tarrytown, NY: Marshall Cavendish, 2002.

Web Sites

▶ **Electronic News**
www.vheadline.com
Venezuela's electronic news site, with current events involving politics, arts, culture, music, and more.

▶ **Embassy of Venezuela in the United States**
www.embavenez-us.org
Web site of the Embassy of the Bolivarian Republic of Venezuela in the United States of America, featuring a variety of information, including a section called "Venezuela for Kids," with such topics as history, geography, sports, and folklore.

▶ **About Venezuela**
www.cia.gov/cia/publications/factbook/geos/ve.html
CIA Web site, listing many facts about Venezuela.

▶ **Your Venezuela**
www.venezuelatuya.com
Tourist portal for Venezuela, featuring a wide variety of facts, photos, and links.

Embassies

▶ **The Venezuelan Embassy in the United States**
1099 30th Street, NW
Washington, D.C. 20007

▶ **The Venezuelan Embassy in Canada**
32 Range Road
Ottawa, Ontario K1N 8J4
Canada

Index

Page numbers in *italics* indicate illustrations.

Meet the Author

T ERRI WILLIS feels that beginning research for a new book feels like the start of a journey. "I spend so much time reading and thinking about the countries as I write about them, I sometimes feel like I'm there," she said.

The journey begins at her local library, where Terri checks out all the materials she can find on a country—books, magazines, videos. She spends several days poring over all the information to get a feel for where she'll be going with the book.

Bookstores often provide more materials. Good travel guides can be very helpful. For her book on Venezuela, Terri particularly enjoyed *Insight Guide: Venezuela*. It contains a lot of great information about the nation and its people, and beautiful photography.

Then Terri heads to the Memorial Library at the University of Wisconsin-Madison. "It's always fun to go back to the campus where I earned my degree," she said. "The library there is full of treasures."

Much of the material from university libraries is very technical and detailed. It takes time to go through the information carefully and present it in a way young people can understand.

The Internet is another good source for material. It's important to use only reliable sources, though, Terri warned. Anybody can create a Web site and put anything on it they want, so not all Internet content is credible. Terri is careful to use only information that comes from such places as universities and government agencies. Even then, she said, it's good to remember that some of these sources may not present the whole picture. A thorough search is important.

Terri fills out her research by talking to people and asking questions. Embassies, chambers of commerce, government agencies, universities—all have knowledgeable people who are willing to help.

Terri has a degree in journalism. Her books include *Libya*, *Romania*, and *Vietnam* in the Enchantment of the World series. Other books for Childrens' Press include *Land Use and Abuse, Cars: an Environmental Challenge* (coauthored by Wallace B. Black), and *Restoring Nature, Land*. She has also edited several books for Children's Press and Raintree Steck Vaughn Publishers.

Terri lives in Cedarburg, Wisconsin, with her husband, Harry, and their two daughters, Andrea and Elizabeth.

Photo Credits

A Perfect Exposure/Gary Braasch: 9 bottom, 41, 116

AP/Wide World Photos: 68, 76 (Jose Caruci), 73 (Douglas Engle), 63 (Fernando Llano), 66, 86 (Dario Lopez-Mills), 18 (Ricardo Mazalan), 98, 102 (Leslie Mazoch), 106 top (Ron Schwane), 106 bottom (John Swart)

Art Resource, NY: 69, 133 bottom (Bolivar Museum, Caracas, Venzuela/Giraudon), 50 (Museu de Arte, Sao Paulo, Brazil/Giraudon)

Bridgeman Art Library International Ltd., London/New York: 44 (Stapleton Collection)

Corbis Images: 115 bottom (AFP), 56 (Stefano Bianchetti), 114 (Geoffrey Clements), 78 top, 118, 123 (Pablo Corral), 103 (Michael Freeman), 113 (Julie Lemberger), 7 bottom, 42 (Douglas Peebles), 83 (Neil Rabinowitz), 110 (Reuters NewMedia Inc.), 53, 59, 115 top

D. Donne Bryant Stock Photography: 92 (John Curtis), 2 (Ed Darack), 111 (Michael Moody), 25, 75, 77 (Chris R. Sharp), cover, 6, 17, 108 (Raul Sojo)

Dembinsky Photo Assoc.: 33 (Tom Boyden), 38 bottom (A.B. Sheldon)

Larry Luxner: 20, 61, 81, 132 bottom

MapQuest.com, Inc.: 65, 131 top

North Wind Picture Archives: 47 bottom

Panos Pictures: 90 (Jerry Callow), 119 (Caroline Penn)

Peter Arnold Inc.: 23 (M. Edwards/Still Pictures), 12 (Jeff Greenberg), 30, 131 bottom (Martin Harvey), 14, 24 (Jacques Janqoux), 80 bottom (Yoram Lehmann), 37 (Luiz C. Marigo), 35 bottom (Roland Seitre)

Photo Researchers, NY: 107 (Carl Frank), 15, 34 bottom, 36, 38 top, 40 top (Francois Gohier), 26, 43, 132 top (Jacques Jangoux), 31 right (Dr. M.P. Kahl), 32 (Jany Sauvanet), 40 bottom right (Karl Weidmann), 121, 127 (Ulrike Welsch), 31 left, 35 top, 39 (Art Wolfe)

South American Pictures: 8, 9 top, 16, 21, 22, 52, 55 top, 86, 87, 88, 120 (Tony Morrison), 99 (Chris Sharp)

Stock Boston: 34 top (John Cancalosi), 72, 74, 104, 105, 112, 122 (Rob Crandall), 125 (Henry Horenstein), 117 (Julie Marzotte), 87 (Mike Mazzaschi), 40 bottom left (Michael Powers), 126, 133 top (David J. Sams)

Stock Montage, Inc.: 47 top, 49 bottom

Superstock, Inc.: 7 top, 13, 27, 70, 130 left

Woodfin Camp & Associates: 96 (G. Clifford), 64, 78 bottom (Mireille Vautier)

Maps by Joe LeMonnier